BUSH NURSES

Annabelle Brayley trained as a registered nurse. She has lived on an isolated sheep and cattle station in Queensland and worked in rural and remote health. After retiring from health to pursue her passion for storytelling, she has become a regular contributor to *RM Williams OUTBACK* magazine. Annabelle lives in the small south-west Queensland community of Morven with her husband, Ian.

BUSH
NURSES

Inspiring true stories of nursing bravery
and ingenuity in rural and remote Australia

Edited by Annabelle Brayley

MICHAEL JOSEPH
an imprint of
PENGUIN BOOKS

MICHAEL JOSEPH

Published by the Penguin Group
Penguin Group (Australia)
707 Collins Street, Melbourne, Victoria 3008, Australia
(a division of Pearson Australia Group Pty Ltd)
Penguin Group (USA) Inc.
375 Hudson Street, New York, New York 10014, USA
Penguin Group (Canada)
90 Eglinton Avenue East, Suite 700, Toronto, Canada ON M4P 2Y3
(a division of Pearson Penguin Canada Inc.)
Penguin Books Ltd
80 Strand, London WC2R 0RL England
Penguin Ireland
25 St Stephen's Green, Dublin 2, Ireland
(a division of Penguin Books Ltd)
Penguin Books India Pvt Ltd
11 Community Centre, Panchsheel Park, New Delhi – 110 017, India
Penguin Group (NZ)
67 Apollo Drive, Rosedale, North Shore 0632, New Zealand
(a division of Pearson New Zealand Ltd)
Penguin Books (South Africa) (Pty) Ltd
Rosebank Office Park, Block D, 181 Jan Smuts Avenue, Parktown North,
Johannesburg, 2196, South Africa
Penguin (Beijing) Ltd
7F, Tower B, Jiaming Center, 27 East Third Ring Road North, Chaoyang District, Beijing 100020, China

Penguin Books Ltd, Registered Offices: 80 Strand, London WC2R 0RL, England

First published by Penguin Group (Australia), 2013

1 3 5 7 9 10 8 6 4 2

Text copyright © this collection Penguin Group (Australia) 2013
Copyright © in individual stories remains with the authors
unless otherwise stated

The moral right of the author has been asserted

Cover design by Alex Ross © Penguin Group (Australia)
Text design by Samantha Jayaweera © Penguin Group (Australia)
Cover photograph 'King Air at Dusk', Royal Flying Doctor Service
Typeset in Sabon by Penguin Group (Australia)
Printed and bound in Australia by McPherson's Printing Group, Maryborough,
Victoria

National Library of Australia
Cataloguing-in-Publication data:

Edited by Brayley, Annabelle.
Bush nurses / Edited by Annabelle Brayley.
9781921901393 (pbk.)
Rural nurses – Australia – Anecdotes.
Nurses – Australia – Anecdotes.
610.73430994

penguin.com.au

CONTENTS

Foreword

'You know what you've got to do. Put a glove on, put your hand in and push the presenting part off the cord so that it can still pulsate. We'll come as soon as we can.'

It was 10.30 at night and I was the District Medical Officer on call for the RFDS in Alice Springs. I was responding to an emergency phone call from a remote area nurse in Ampilatwatja, 270 kilometres north-east of Alice Springs. She had a woman in established labour with a cord prolapse.

With the assistance of a local traditional Aboriginal midwife, she managed to give the woman some pethidine, put her on oxygen, got her to crouch on her elbows and knees on a bed and inserted her gloved hand into her birth canal. Holding the baby's head off the cord enabled lifesaving oxygenated blood to continue to flow to the baby.

Meanwhile, back in Alice Springs, we had taken off in a Navajo and were about ten minutes in the air when a safety light indicated the door hadn't closed properly. As per safety protocol we returned to base to check it out, delaying our departure for another agonising forty minutes. It was over two hours before we finally arrived in the community. I doubted the baby would be alive. At the clinic we found an exhausted nurse still in position and feeling paralysed from her fingers to her neck. I asked if she could feel a pulse in the cord but she was past feeling anything. When I listened with the Sonic-Aid, there it was: *kathump . . . kathump . . . kathump*. The baby was alive!

We got everything ready for a delivery and resuscitation. I still doubted the baby would survive but I phoned the paediatrician on call in Alice Springs hospital to warn him to be ready for a very sick baby. Then I said to the nurse, 'You take your hand out and I'll put mine in,' which we did, and I discovered that the cervix was fully dilated and the baby's head was well down. We turned the woman over onto her back and got her to push, and in less than a minute there was a very flat but alive baby on the bed. With a bit of help the baby was soon crying; it was wonderful!

We got back to Alice Springs about 4.30 a.m. with a perfect baby and a happy mother and the paediatric staff waiting for us wondering what all the fuss was about. Next afternoon I rang the nurse at the community and asked how she was. She said, 'After the plane took off, I helped put out the flares and then went back and cleaned up the clinic and got to bed about 4 a.m. At 6 a.m. someone knocked on my door asking for Panadol.' That's remote area nursing. Nobody in the community seemed to realise the magnitude of what she had done – she had saved the life of that baby and was still on call for everyone else.

Working in remote health is a huge challenge, one that I first became familiar with as a fifth-year medical student on an elective in the Southern Highlands of Papua New Guinea. During my time there, I delivered my first babies and learnt how to resuscitate newborns from the community midwife; learnt to cross-match blood under paraffin lamplight from a

Pidgin-speaking health worker; and how to do lumbar punctures and set up external fixation of femoral fractures from local nurses. It was a 'see one, do one, teach one' school of medicine. I saw amazing things and gained many invaluable skills, and all from nurses and community health workers. It was a life-changing experience.

Six years in rural Africa as a young doctor further reinforced the fact that nothing is to be gained from keeping knowledge and skills 'secret' from any clinical staff. I learnt how to deliver breeches and do vacuum extractions from highly experienced midwives, and performed craniotomies and laparotomies under the guidance of a Russian trained Nepali surgeon. Sharing knowledge and skills across professional boundaries and traditional scopes of practice was essential to the way you worked in Third World situations. There was no room for professional hierarchies and egos.

When I came back to Australia I worked as a District Medical Officer in Alice Springs for eight years. As a result of my experiences in PNG and Africa, I was able to help establish the CARPA (Central Australian Rural Practitioners Association) Standard Treatment manual. It has become the 'bible' for remote area staff and, together with the CRANA*plus* procedures manual, demystifies emergency treatment and procedures, as is illustrated by another remote health story.

I was flying out to a single-vehicle rollover near Uluru. There was a nurse from Imanpa, a nearby Aboriginal community, who'd gone as first responder. I was able to talk to her on a satellite phone newly installed on the RFDS plane. She'd done the right thing and left the person in the car because he was a query spinal injury. He also had an obvious chest injury, judging from her description of the skin over his chest feeling 'crackly', indicating an air leak from a pneumothorax. She'd put an IV line in and a neck collar on, put him on oxygen and given him pain relief. She was on her own. We flew over the scene but couldn't land and had to fly to a nearby cattle station and drive back. As we were flying over, the nurse reported via the sat phone that the patient had deteriorated and was very distressed, and she could no longer feel a pulse. I said, 'You have to shove a needle in his chest.' She'd never done anything like that. I said, 'Just shove a needle in over where the chest is crackling.' She said, 'Oh, oh, oh . . . ' and then the line went dead. Once we landed it took another twenty minutes to get to the accident scene, where the nurse was standing with an expression somewhere between terror and triumph on her face. The man had a 16 gram needle sticking out of his chest and was alive. She had saved his life. Without that needle he'd have been dead from a tension pneumothorax.

There are lots of stories like this . . . and this book is full of them. Some will raise the hairs on the back of your neck, some will make you laugh, and some will make you cry. Others will tell you how it just is or has been, as the stories range across a century of nursing in rural and remote areas of Australia.

There used to be a standing joke that if you were a nurse and 'had a pulse' you could work in remote health services. That was never true, but it is true that the further away you are from metropolitan areas, the more likely it is that a nurse will be the most experienced health practitioner. Rural and remote areas have always relied on the character and skill of nurses, and will continue to do so. Well-resourced and well-supported advanced-practice nurse practitioners, training and working within genuine multidisciplinary team environments, are the future. As you read this book you will realise that the nurses and health practitioners who choose to work 'out there' are well up for it.

Dr Nicholas Williams
MBBS, DRACOG
MSc(PHC), FAFPHM, FACRRM

Introduction

When I was young and growing up in rural Queensland, I really wanted to be a hairdresser. However, my father thought young women should be nurses or teachers. So it was that I trained as a nurse. Obviously anyone can train for anything; however, true nurses are born rescuers and nurturers and either you are one or you're not. From the beginning, I regularly got into trouble for sitting on beds talking with the patients and listening to their stories, a predilection which ultimately led to the role I undertake now as a storyteller. Happily for all concerned back then, when I finished my training, I got a job as a receptionist with a shearing contractor!

Having started my training at Princess Alexandra Hospital in Brisbane, I finished it on a regional training program out of Charleville Base Hospital in south-west Queensland. The first thing that struck me in Charleville was how much broader my scope for practical learning was going to be. In a big city hospital, as a nurse, you often have to be in exactly the right place at exactly the right time to experience some of the really interesting incidents and challenges. And even then you'd have the luxury of more qualified people right there beside you to back you up. In the bush, as often as not, you're it; you're on your own. That's a sentiment reflected in this book by more than one very highly qualified city nurse who headed to the outback for an adventure and found themselves floundering and uncertain.

These stories span a century of nursing in rural and remote areas and cover a broad range of experiences. Over the weeks and months of collecting and editing these stories, I have worked some days with tears streaming down my face; other days I have howled with laughter. Every day, I've been humbled by extraordinary stories of bravery, courage, determination, motivation, commitment, comedy and tragedy, interwoven with the theme of ordinary people doing ordinary everyday things to ensure the primary health and wellbeing of their fellow man.

Nurses, as a breed, are generally taken for granted. Bush nurses are not only taken for granted, but they are also often completely overlooked, and yet the bush has traditionally run on nurse power. Not only do they nurse, but many of them also sell tickets in raffles, bake cakes for sake stalls, volunteer at sports events and help organise functions, all while keeping a watching brief on their communities. Nurses are often the lynchpins around which their communities revolve. Bush nurses are generally self-assured, creative and dedicated. In addition, most nurses who work remotely are highly experienced, innovative, resourceful and multi-skilled. By virtue of their isolation, they have to be.

Without doubt, we need more doctors in rural and remote areas. There are some things only a doctor can do. But the best doctors anywhere are those who recognise the value of collaboration; who understand that standing apart from multidisciplinary solutions is counter-productive; who understand that their good outcomes often rest on the first response and preparation that was administered by a nurse.

And before any rural and remote ambulance officers and paramedics jump up and down about just who first responders are, you are represented here by Mick Lanagan, a volunteer ambo who's the guardian of the Great Northern Highway in Western Australia. There's also a couple of Aboriginal health practitioners, a couple of student nurses, a retired nurse who voluntarily ran the clinic in her community for decades, a carer and a whole gamut of nurses including registered nurses and midwives, both with and without remote area experience.

Bush Nurses is a celebration of all those who 'nurse' those of us who live in the inland of Australia.

Annabelle Brayley

chapter one
BABY BUSINESS

One thing about babies is, once they're in there, they have to come out. The when, how and where provide the foundations of these stories about babies and the midwives who delivered them, sometimes under the most difficult circumstances, but always with the anticipatory joy of welcoming new life.

Miracle Birth
CENTRAL QUEENSLAND

I am retired now, but I nursed for twenty years. Most of my nursing career was in the rural sector as I enjoyed the variety of doing a bit of everything, as opposed to at a large metropolitan hospital and having to choose your speciality. I also enjoyed the laidback attitude and knowing the people you were dealing with. I cannot go any further without mentioning those wonderful country morning teas made by the kitchen staff. Nothing would beat fresh scones with jam and cream after a busy morning. Of course, when the bureaucrats used to come, gone were the good things and out came the two-in-the-packet, Arnott's finest selection.

The story I'd like to share with you is one I definitely experienced personally. I was expecting my third child. Because we lived in the country, I was driving two hours to see the doctor as I was determined to have my baby in a private hospital in a larger centre. I had a thing about not having babies where I worked. It was something I vowed I would never do. After one particular visit with the obstetrician and feeling quite deflated and not at all empowered about my impending birth plan, I wanted to know why rural ladies could not be under midwives. After all, being one myself, I understand that they can offer a totally different approach to birthing.

I had discussed things with my husband and realised that, if I did in fact deliver in our local hospital, it would be advantageous as he wouldn't have to be away from the property for any length of time. Also, caring for two boys three and under would be much more achievable at home. As I was working at the time of this revelation, I walked into the director of nursing's office at our small hospital and asked her if she would consent to being my midwife. She agreed and then spoke with our medical superintendent, who reluctantly agreed. The deal was I had to have so many visits with him as well.

After that decision had been made, it felt like a huge load had been lifted from me. For the first time ever I felt that, if for some reason my husband couldn't be there, I was comfortable enough that my friend and colleague would act on my behalf and do the best for both myself and my baby, and I could just get on with the job of doing the hard yards.

When the big day actually came, we didn't realise it at first. Three weeks out from my due date my husband and I headed off to Bundaberg, four hours away, to do the last-minute shop and purchase a new vehicle. Arriving there at 9 o'clock at night after stopping along the way a few times for my Braxton Hicks contractions, we then spent time catching up with my husband's sister. Finally, at midnight we climbed into bed only to be rudely awakened by my waters breaking (something that had never happened in my previous births) an hour later. I woke my husband and told him we had to go home as I was going to have a baby. I phoned my midwife and told her I wasn't contracting so I was coming home to have this baby with the people I felt safe and comfortable with. After uttering an expletive upon finding out where we were and that we were four hours away, she said, 'Ring me when you get here!'

With that we were off and just like in the movies, it was cold and raining. All my husband could think (he confessed later) was, *Every hospital we are passing is getting smaller!* We arrived home in the early hours of the morning to a startled set of grandparents who were told, in answer to their question, 'What's happening?', that, 'We're having a baby!' My colleague came out and did a home visit and checked all was okay.

It was a strange labour, lots of stopping and starting, but eventually things progressed enough to head into hospital to have the baby. It could not have worked out any better, as my backup midwife happened to be working and a nurse I had total confidence in was there as well.

Then came the interesting bit. The labour progressed, but it was quite different from what I had previously experienced.

I finally started to push and delivered a baby boy but something was *very* different. I couldn't move and there was no sense of that relief you have after the baby is born. The whole world seemed to slow down and my recollection of events is as clear now as it was in the room that night. Right at that moment when the placenta is supposed to come out I thought, *Gee, this is a big placenta*, and just as I thought this, my mind registered that it wasn't a placenta at all. It was, in fact, another baby! Simultaneously my midwife said, 'Judi, don't do this to me!' All I could think was, *Like I have any control!* Clear thoughts like, *No need to panic, we can just hold onto this baby until the placenta comes away*, and *We don't need extra clamps*, came into mind and I couldn't quite believe how calm I was. It was a very surreal moment and there wasn't a dry eye in the room!

The next challenge was to get people to believe that we had really had twins. My husband is known as a bit of a practical joker and had been telling people there were two in there. He joked to people afterwards that I had had the choice of ticking a box: one was one baby at twelve pounds and the other was two at six pounds each. He told anyone who would listen that I ticked the second box. Even my mother wouldn't believe him until she came in and saw them for herself.

My plans of coming in, having a baby, then going home were totally thrown out the window. Fortunately they were a healthy size and took to feeding like ducks to water. Finally, a week later we were allowed to take them home. Our med super had a firm word to my husband about the need to look after his new precious cargo. We now had four under four – all boys.

Their births were an absolute miracle, and as a midwife it never ceases to amaze me seeing new life come into this world. From an analytical point of view it could be perceived as a near miss. Sometimes it is nice to be reminded, though, that women were created to have babies.

The feeling of warmth and security, knowing exactly who was assisting me in the birthing suit, I am sure contributed to the safe arrival of those boys. My other colleagues, who would bring me tea and toast in the middle of the night if I were up feeding, created a bond that is still strong to this day. Finally, to know that my husband didn't have to travel vast distances to see me and that our other children were able to sleep in their own beds was totally worth it.

Judi Bain, registered nurse and midwife

Cyclone Baby

I guess when you have been nursing as long as I have, you will have heard many myths about emergencies in the middle of storms, especially in the midwifery field.

In 2008, I was the nurse practitioner and sole nurse at the Marble Bar Clinic in north-west Western Australia. We received news around 5 p.m. that Cyclone George was bearing down on us. We had been aware of the path for some time and our town plan had been activated.

My job was to stay in the clinic and anyone injured or in trouble would be brought into me by police or FESA (Fire and Emergency Services Authority).

The clinic had survived cyclones before so I bunked down there feeling I'd be safe, even if a bit wet. We had gone onto red alert and the winds were screaming in at 125 kilometres per hour. The clinic, while withstanding the wind, was old and a few (too many) leaks developed with the horizontal rain.

At around 6 p.m., I received a call from a station about 50 kilometres out on the gravel road to Nullagine to say that a woman had gone into labour. Protocol was that women at thirty-six to thirty-seven weeks stayed in Port Hedland. This woman, who had reportedly just come visiting, was unknown to me. The station contact stated she was a Gravida 5 Para 4 (meaning this was her fifth pregnancy and she had already delivered four full-term babies, so it all might happen quite quickly) and she was due in one week.

As the manager of the station could not leave there, he wanted me to retrieve her. He had numerous families to protect on the station. So I made a bargain that I would come and meet them if they started driving her in. I contacted the police, who at this time were evacuating the local Aboriginal community, to see if they could provide a driver to come with me. No. I then contacted the local FESA for assistance. The local captain, Leona, agreed to come with me.

We set off into the wind, finding ourselves almost leaning forward to assist the troopy 4WD's forward movement. It was dark, black, wet and windy. Eventually we met the station car on the gravel road some 25 kilometres from Marble Bar. Both cars stopped close together and the four men in the station vehicle got out, opened the back of the troopy and literally lifted the lady onto the stretcher. I hopped in the back as well, then they heaved the doors closed and drove away, keen to get back to the station.

Leona got into the driver's seat and we both looked at each other a bit fearfully, as the troopy was tending to sway sideways in the wind. A cursory glance at the mother made me readjust my thinking. Her toes were curling with her pains and she looked like she meant business. I asked Leona to wait a moment while I examined her as best I could. When I got to the working end there was a little cap of hair waiting for me. Leona went to get out, to come and help me, but we decided that was not a good idea as the doors would probably pull out of her grip.

So she climbed from the front to the back, getting there just in time to receive the delivered child in our confined space. While I proceeded to go through assisting the work of third stage, Leona got the child settled with mum.

I am not sure if we were as aware of our movements and delivery as we were of the swaying troopy. However, all done, Leona crawled back into the front, turned the troopy slowly and headed back to Marble Bar. In contrast to our trip out, we were almost blown back. The mother spent two days at the clinic before she could be flown out. Mother and baby girl were both fine. I have never forgotten that night, and Leona in the ensuing years has gone on to become a registered nurse.

The joys of remote work are so rewarding. Your results are in front of you at all times. Sometimes you have to go about delivering the service in a different way, but what a way to get paid for having fun, doing what you do best.

Chris Haar, registered nurse, midwife

Baby Magic
NORTHERN TERRITORY

I was working in a community in west Arnhem Land in February 1999; I'd been there for about twelve months. There was a young girl there who wanted to be pregnant, though she was a bit younger than we'd have liked, being only fifteen or sixteen years old. She came from a family of heavy drinkers but didn't drink or do drugs, and otherwise did everything right to make her pregnancy safe and viable. She just wanted to be pregnant, did all the right things and had turned up regularly for antenatal care. She had a good-size baby and everything went according to plan. We transferred our ladies out to Darwin at thirty-eight weeks for birthing; she was only a couple of days off going out and everything was going well when she went into spontaneous labour.

I am a midwife, as was one of my other colleagues, and the process was that we did the assessments and talked to the district medical officer in Darwin. Because she was at term and it was a first baby, we didn't do anything to stop labour and she just chooffed along doing all the right things as labouring ladies do.

The retrieval aircraft was coming and actually got to within ten minutes of us when they had a call-out to another delivery of twins, about as far away from us as they could go and still be in our health district. The DMO rang us explaining the situation and because our lady was well within the normal parameters of first stage of labour, the decision was made to divert to the twins, who were only at twenty-four weeks gestation. The aircraft turned around and went back the other way, which meant we wouldn't be able to transfer for several hours. We weren't concerned about that at all; all was going according to plan.

The labour progressed and the young lady became a little distressed as some women do. She was tired and a bit agitated and a bit over it, as happens when you're several hours into the whole thing. We had her cannulated as was normal in the circumstances and we got to the stage where, on examination, the baby was head down as it should have been. However, things didn't seem quite right, though we couldn't quite work out why.

She'd got to the stage where she was totally over it, she didn't want to be there, she wanted the baby born *now*, she wanted more pain relief and she wanted to run away. She got quite anxious and bit one of the staff. Her grandmothers, who were there supporting her, told her off. She proceeded to rip out the IV cannulas and then she did run away, despite us and her grandmothers telling her it wouldn't change anything; the baby still had to come out!

Next thing her husband brought her back and she wouldn't let him leave. He put her down on the bed and she clung onto his arm. In this community there was this whole thing around women's business and usually the mother would come with supporting women, in this case her grandmothers, and usually there wasn't a moment when they were not touching her and talking to her to help her through the delivery. Men were not a 'normal' part of the birthing picture. But anyway, he stayed with her, which was lovely, and he was there when she delivered a perfectly normal baby. The thing is, it was the first time, in my experience, that an Aboriginal man had been there for the delivery of his child.

The look of wonderment on his face was just magic and serves to constantly remind me of the privilege that is given to me, being involved in a family's birth.

Monica Ostigh, registered nurse and midwife
(remote area nurse)

New Life

KALTUKATJARA (DOCKER RIVER),
NORTHERN TERRITORY

The policy in remote Australia is that all pregnant women go to a main centre such as Alice Springs at thirty-eight weeks gestation for 'sit down', to stay at a hostel until their baby is born. Federal funding pays for their travel in and out once baby is born, and for two weeks' accommodation, extended by another two weeks if warranted. Only if it is a first baby is there funding to pay for an escort, company while you wait out those last few days and weeks.

Many women have no-one to leave their other children with. They worry that their husband will be lonely for them, and maybe have an affair while they are gone. There is often no family in town to sit with them and visit during the day. They may have no money as their benefits are going back to their other children, back at home. It can be a long, lonely waiting time, punctuated by antenatal visits to strangers they are meeting for the first time.

Many of the women in remote areas of Australia suffer from compromised general health, including illnesses such as diabetes, sexually transmitted diseases and rheumatic heart disease. These put them in a higher risk category when it comes to medical management of pregnancy and birth. Women want healthy babies and don't wish to put themselves and their baby at risk.

English may be the third, fourth or fifth language of these

women, and interpreters are a rarity rather than part of routine health care. Even simple explanations give women more information to make a better-informed choice about how they wish to manage their conception, pregnancy and birth. Under current government policy, choice regarding place of birth is denied to women living in remote Australia.

Every year there are women who choose not to access health care during pregnancy or who present late for the birth of their baby. The most important factor in enabling women to access care during pregnancy and birth is the trust they have in their health care professional. Once trust is established, care can be delivered in many ways. Flexibility is required on both sides.

One girl was so shy about being pregnant and coming to the clinic, the midwife, who was also the RAN, used to go to her house, on a Friday afternoon when it was all quiet and no-one was there, for her antenatal checks. The girl went to 'sit down' but returned before the birth of her baby; she was lonely and scared. She came to tell the midwife and then returned again for 'sit down' having been able to touch base with her family.

Another woman refused to believe she was pregnant when the test was positive on a routine health screen. For many months she kept insisting she had gallstones (as she had seen them on an X-ray) and wasn't pregnant, but happily came for all her antenatal checks. At about thirty-two weeks gestation she decided she was having a baby and wanted to have it in the community. This was a community that had no night evacuation facilities and at that time only one RAN, who was also a midwife. She was carrying a large baby and hadn't gone for any scans – as she wasn't pregnant and had already seen her gallstones on an X-ray! The RAN talked to her about the risks and she went to 'sit down', eventually birthing a son.

On another occasion the RAN was called out at about 11 p.m. by a community woman who said she had a severe pain in her face. Several women were attending, one of whom was heavily pregnant and sat on her seat squirming and fidgeting as the RAN looked at the woman who had called her out. Nothing wrong with her face; the pregnant lady was in labour and a baby was born in the early hours of the morning.

Babies born to healthy mothers in the community generally remained in the clinic for twenty-four hours. They then went home and received daily visits from the RAN for about three days and after that were brought by their mothers to the clinic for review. With only one RAN on site, this was extremely tiring, as other community members did not stop being ill because a baby had been born. However, those babies and mothers did much better than those born away from family support and their community.

On one home visit, to see a new baby less than forty-eight hours old, the RAN saw the baby's three-year-old cousin, leaning over it and giving it a big hug. The cousin was covered in active chicken pox sores. The RAN was sleep deprived, having had only three hours' sleep since the baby's birth. She wandered back to the clinic, thinking, 'I know there is something bad about chicken pox and babies, I had better ring the doctor on call.' The doctor on call was very casual, saying, 'I don't think it is a big concern but I will ring the paediatrician.'

Two minutes later the phone rang with a frantic doctor on the line. If the baby showed the slightest symptoms of being unwell it needed to be evacuated immediately and in the meantime, how fast could we get some immunoglobin? The Alice Springs hospital had some immunoglobin in its pharmacy; however, release had to be authorised by a senior doctor in Darwin.

As usual, these fusses happen on Friday afternoons. Luckily the RAN's husband was in Alice Springs and was able to collect the immunoglobin from the pharmacy and drive home, an eight-hour road trip. As soon as he arrived the immunoglobin was drawn up and injected into the baby. Later blood tests showed the mother was non-immune so had no protective antibodies to pass on through breast milk. The other children in the house caught chicken pox from each other, but the baby remained chicken pox-free and grew up into a happy, healthy girl.

Women in remote Australia need appropriate information so they can make informed choices about conception, pregnancy and birth. They also need support in the choices they make, rather than being blamed or treated differently because they don't wish to follow the one-size-fits-all policy of the health department. Healthy babies can be born in remote settings; women need access to skilled practitioners who can provide good perinatal care and support women with accurate information regarding possibilities and risks. Health care professionals also need to be supported in the care they provide, so that adequate staffing levels are available and women can receive care from health professionals not distracted through sleep deprivation or with other health needs.

Lyn Byers, midwife, nurse practitioner
(remote area nurse)

Stepping Up

COOBER PEDY, SOUTH AUSTRALIA

When I first started working as a missionary nurse with the Bush Church Aid Society in 1971, I was sent to relieve, for two weeks, in the opal mining town of Coober Pedy in South Australia. Without a doctor in the town, we relied our own medical knowledge, although we could always telephone or radio the Flying Doctor at Port Augusta for advice, and one of them did a weekly visit to Coober Pedy. In many ways we were very much alone and I thought I would never cope. However, after two years working at Cook, on the Trans Australian rail link halfway across the Nullarbor, and Laverton, another mining town in Western Australia, I was much more confident.

Originally there had only been two nurses at Coober Pedy, but on my return in 1973 there were now four of us working at the hospital: one doing outpatients, one doing inpatients and helping with outpatients, one in charge of the domestic scene and the fourth one off duty. We also had some help here with the cleaning and hospital washing by employing local workers. All the cooking was done by us and my cooking was still not brilliant, but I managed.

After my initial feelings of inadequacy two years prior, now I suddenly found the medical work in Coober Pedy intriguing. It was no secret that midwifery was my favourite and when I heard there was a mid in, it took all my resolve to stay out of it, even when I was on my days off. One day, a French lady presented in early labour with her first babe. As a rule, we never delivered first babies in the outback because the mothers had no previous obstetric history. This lady had been booked to go to Port Augusta a month before her due date. She was just about to embark on that journey when the labour started, and she presented at the hospital. 'I will not interfere unless asked,' I said to myself, but God already knew how much I wanted to be involved and provided me the ability to achieve.

The plane was sent for and when it arrived the mother was in such good labour that the plane turned back. Much more dangerous to deliver mid-air, it was decided. Not long after, the labour became obstructed, and we had a real dilemma on our hands. 'Would you be able to do a forceps, Audrey?' Carol asked. I thought, *Would I? Just give me the chance!* I had assisted with many and knew the procedure off by heart. The flying doctor spoke to me by phone. 'Whatever you do, don't pull hard,' he said. But he gave me permission to go ahead.

Gowned and gloved, I assessed the situation. The membranes were ruptured, the patient in labour, the bladder and bowel empty, the cervix fully dilated, the foetal heart present but dropping, and there was no time to lose. We explained to this lady that this was not usually our job, but in her case there was no other safe option. She gave her consent. I checked the position of the presenting part. Thank God it was a head, but which way was it lying? I had examined many women in labour but never with the head down so low. The feeling was quite foreign to my fingers as I searched for some recognisable marker. Suddenly I had it – a tiny ear on the upper side, to the patient's right. I now knew that this baby was in the best position for a successful forceps delivery.

I cut the episiotomy as I had done so many times as a

staff midwife at the Royal Women's Hospital in Melbourne. The forceps lubricated, I gently inserted them one at a time, as I had seen done countless times before, but they didn't fit together and I knew they must before I could proceed. I took them off and tried again. This time a perfect fit and I knew I was ready. The next contraction came but I remembered the doctor's words so I didn't pull. Nothing happened.

Babies are tough when coming through the birth canal and when the passage is a bit narrow, as it was in this case, as long as the position of the head is safe and the forceps application is correct, I knew that more pressure could and must be applied to save the baby. The baby's heart rate was slowing and I knew there was no longer any choice. The next contraction had to be it so, when it came, I pulled with all my might, successfully extracting quite a blue little babe.

A quick assessment told me she may never breathe without some kind of intervention. I was comforted by the wise words of Dr Glynn White, one of my lecturers when I was doing Infant Welfare in Melbourne. 'All you need is oxygen and suction . . .' he'd said.

I complied, and with the help of frog breathing, another trick I'd learnt in my training days, I resuscitated the babe to a pink, screaming bundle and turned to deliver the afterbirth and sew up the episiotomy. The whole process was a tremendous blessing, not the least of it being that there was not a single forceps mark on the baby's face. What a miracle. A year later, the parents brought their little girl back to see us. There she was, fit, healthy and meeting all her milestones.

Audrey Aspeling, retired registered nurse and midwife

The Arrival of Annabelle ...

NORTH-WEST QUEENSLAND

It was Sunday afternoon on 9 September 1988 and we were at home on our cattle and sheep station 160 kilometres south-west of Mount Isa, and everyone was busy getting ready for the annual shearing. We didn't have a two-way radio. My mum, an art teacher, was up visiting from Sydney to help for two weeks.

Our fourth child, who was due in two days, was in a hurry! My waters broke and contractions began at about four minutes apart. I called my friend and neighbour Mandy to ask if she would take me in to Mount Isa when I got to her place. So with help from Mum and our nine-year-old daughter, Belinda, we bundled the other two kids into the wagon and headed off to Mandy's house, 40 kilometres down the dirt road. Eager to help, Mum said she'd drive, but by the time we reached the mailbox 2 kilometres down the road and ten long minutes later, I declared that I'd drive because I'd be quicker.

Driving up over the ridge to Mandy's turnoff, I breathed a sigh of relief to see Mandy waiting for me, followed by a much bigger sigh and prayer of thanks when I realised she wasn't alone. Bless my friend; she had called the local bush nurse at Dajarra. This wonderful grandma, Lesley, was waiting to help us; with her husband Norm driving the ambulance parked beside them, they were ready to take us to Mount Isa. I asked Belinda to drive Mum and the other two kids home and climbed into the back of the ambulance with a sense of peace, even though I knew our baby was in the breech position and that things could get tricky!

Lesley examined me and promptly asked Norm to step on it because this baby was well on its way to being born. Then she told me that an ambulance from Mount Isa was on its way to do a halfway meet so she and Norm could return to Dajarra as soon as possible, but that there was no way she was going to hand us over; she promised to be with us all the way and that the other ambulance could follow them back to Mount Isa! Lesley admitted that neither she nor Donna, the Mount Isa nurse, had ever delivered a breech baby but that didn't matter because our Lord was watching over us all.

The sun was getting low on the horizon and all the cattle and roos for miles around were on the move looking for a feed. Many of them were searching the roadside for grass to munch on, so we travelled slowly to avoid a collision with them.

It was tough going with contractions every minute or so; agony and sweat followed by a very short reprieve. Lesley lovingly cared for us and encouraged me. Her touch was gentle, her voice soft and calm even when she told me off for not already being in town for the past three weeks! She understood my dilemma: me wanting desperately to help my husband to get ready for shearing; three kids to care for; a governess too vacant for words and my lovely mum no help at all.

We met the Mount Isa ambulance and they were told to follow behind us. We were very nearly there, only 20 kilometres to Mount Isa, just rounding the bend to cross over Sybella Creek, when our baby decided it was time to join the world!

Norm pulled off the side of the road as we began our first push. Lesley held my hand and wiped my forehead as Donna opened up the ambulance doors to join us.

This was agony beyond belief; our baby was presenting one foot and one knee, time and time again! What to do? Norm had called Mount Isa hospital for a doctor to come out and help, but that would take time we didn't have! One more contraction, a flood of agony, and I screamed out at the top of my lungs, 'God help me!' As I called out, Lesley says she heard God tell her to put her hand inside me, push back the knee and pull out the hidden foot before the next contraction.

With no time to waste, Lesley told Donna to move and did as she was told just as the next contraction gripped me. Out slithered our baby's feet, legs, body, shoulders and arms, with only her head to follow. Lesley and Donna were pleased but frowns still crowded their faces. A flood of relief swept over me just as the next contraction gripped me. Three, four, five contractions followed one on top of the other but our little girl's head remained stuck.

We were all struggling when Lesley realised that she had to get my bottom high up off the bed. One more contraction and still no head; I was lifted higher still as she gently pleaded with me. Exhausted and terrified, we managed to lift my bottom higher still as the next contraction overwhelmed me and our little girl's head slipped out. I collapsed back, trembling with exhaustion and excitement, but only for a split second because, as I looked over at Lesley and Donna, I saw that their faces were etched with grave concern and desperation.

I asked how our little girl was and was told that she had died. Working deftly, they quickly cut her umbilical cord.

Donna then laid our little girl across Lesley's knees and she began cardiac massage. As Norm placed the tiny oxygen mask over her tiny porcelain white face to give her some much-needed air, Lesley told him quietly that only 100 per cent oxygen would do.

Pleading desperately in my mind, I told God that we loved this little girl He had given us and would be delighted to be able to raise her but that, if He needed to take her home, then we would accept His will. All was deathly quiet as Lesley and Norm did their jobs.

Finally a slight shadow of pink began to wash out the porcelain white in her tiny face. We all looked at each other in wonder and thankfulness as the pink flooded her little body and finally she began to try to wriggle and cry. Time to take stock; check for a pulse and the steady rise and fall of her chest. *Yes*, our Annabelle Lesley was alive!

Thank you, God, and His faithful nurse Lesley. Bless you, Lesley!

Pip Hacon, mother and grazier's wife

Postscript: Annabelle is now twenty-four-years old, married to a lovely bloke, lives in Toowoomba and thoroughly enjoys her job as a registered nurse in Accident and Emergency at Toowoomba Base hospital.

The Magic of Midwifery

THE RIVERINA, NEW SOUTH WALES

Being a midwife is an amazing vocation. Birth is a miracle and to assist women to give birth and care for their new baby is an unbelievable privilege. My hospital is a major referral centre for a large region in rural NSW. Our catchment runs to the west, south-west and north-west for more than 300 kilometres across the plains, to the east 150 kilometres or more in the mountains. Currently 850 babies per year are born in the area, but one year recently there were 926 babies.

Many of the women we help are high risk, transferred from smaller bush hospitals and isolated areas. Some women are actively labouring on arrival. We are expected to be multi-skilled and have the ability to work in each area, from the midwives clinic to the birth suite, and the special care nursery. We work in antenatal and postnatal areas and, when necessary, give phone triage advice.

Every day I am challenged; every day I learn something new and not one day goes by when there has not been something to interest and/or amuse me and my colleagues.

A young doctor who worked some gruelling overtime hours went home dog-tired. He thought his wife had left him a stew in the refrigerator and he ate it. Next day he discovered that he had eaten the cat food. We thought he might come to work meowing.

A few years ago a woman presented to our office and said to the midwife, 'I am here to be "seduced" by Dr L.' Dr L was a well-respected doctor who had been in practice for many years. The midwife had trouble not laughing. She knew that Dr L was planning to 'induce' the woman's labour.

The midwife's sense of humour often carries her through the plain hard work on a shift. Her ability to remain calm and focused is important in an emergency situation. Midwives support each other in the difficult times and the good times. They deal with a balancing act created by the need to care for pregnant teenagers, older first-time mothers, expectant women from isolated areas, high-risk women with multiple medical problems, and women who give birth with apparent ease.

Midwives never know what situation is going to walk through the door and what they will have to deal with in any one shift. The challenging and the unexpected problems keep them on their toes and keep their brains stimulated beyond their wildest dreams. They need to make rapid assessments when there is a deviation from normal, and involve the doctor promptly as time can make a difference.

Life in the maternity unit can be either a feast or a famine. On one memorable occasion, we had ten babies arrive in three and a half hours. The first arrived at 1 a.m. and the last at 4.30 a.m. Extra midwives and a GP with obstetric qualifications were called in to assist in the birth explosion. Every room was taken, corridors were lined with people and one baby was delivered in the waiting room. Despite the sudden influx of babies there were no complications with any of the deliveries.

Triage telephone calls are a lifeline to expectant mothers and are treated seriously. Each call is documented and recorded for later reference. One such call was from a first-time expectant mother who was carrying twins. At thirty-one weeks she went into threatened premature labour, her waters broke and she had occasional contractions. She lived more than an hour's drive from the hospital where she was booked to give birth and was very distraught when she phoned. The very first thing I said was that she needed to calm down for the sake of herself and her unborn babies, and then I reassured her that everything would be all right. I collected the details and suggested she phone 000 for an ambulance, and assured her the staff would be waiting for her to assess her labour. The woman lived in the mountains to the east and, at night, kangaroos were a serious road hazard.

Eventually the expectant mother and father arrived, her labour was stabilised and she was flown north to the nearest tertiary care hospital with neonatal intensive care beds. That day she gave birth to a girl and a boy, and they were later returned to our special care nursery till they had grown and were feeding well. The new mother told me that my words reminding her to calm down for the sake of her babies, and my reassurance, were the most important things she heard that night. She was able focus on keeping her babies inside as long as possible rather than going out of control with fear.

One of the most important rules that I live by is to follow my gut feelings and to listen to the mother. One of my two daughters had four babies, felt very well during each pregnancy and gave birth without any problems. When she became pregnant with her fifth child she would say to me, 'Mum, this baby is going to die before I can push it out.' I heard these words on a regular basis. Her protection instinct was alert all the time.

Towards the end of her pregnancy she phoned me to say

that the baby was hardly moving. I told her to go to her local hospital and have the midwives monitor the baby. She did so but remained anxious, so I phoned a tertiary centre some distance away and discussed the issue with the antenatal clinic there. They were very concerned at the history I gave them. They assessed her and the birth was induced. The little girl was a scrawny baby with little fat on her body. When the umbilical cord was checked they found two true knots in it, which had cut off nutrients during her development. In the opinion of the obstetric team, had she been left another day she would have died. Today I have a vibrant granddaughter named Meg Louise Grace. She was named Grace as her mother and I believe that it was only by the grace of God that she survived the journey of pregnancy.

Apart from some women presenting with a phantom pregnancy and thinking they are in labour, cryptic pregnancies are not uncommon. A young woman who lived in the country, had never been pregnant and had had no period for three years, was being treated by a naturopath for 'liver failure' and 'ascitis' (excessive fluid in the abdominal cavity). Her condition seemed to worsen, she continued to gain weight, experienced air bubbles and movement in her stomach and felt generally unwell, despite having a liver cleanse and other naturopathic treatments. She went to her local doctor who diagnosed her as thirty-seven weeks pregnant, and three weeks later she gave birth to a beautiful baby girl. Her husband was very excited about the results of his wife's worsening condition!

Another woman who did not know she was pregnant went to her doctor after three days of diarrhoea and pains. He sent her to the maternity unit, as she was 5 centimetres dilated with bulging membranes. She obviously had had no antenatal care as she did not know she was pregnant. Initially, when the doctor phoned, he thought she may have only been twenty-eight weeks pregnant. It was estimated that she was actually close to time as her baby was well developed.

All experienced midwives have attended many memorable births, and often women see you in the supermarket and recount their birth experience to you and remember the role you played in their lives. Many keep me informed of the progress of the child I assisted into the world, and I am invited to various family events and milestones of that child or adult.

I was the midwife for my younger daughter Mary-Jo and assisted her to give birth to her daughter Hannah-Rose and her son Andrew. They are two births that remain etched in my memory. These children continue to remind me that I am their Mama and their midwife. There is a special bond between us.

Every birth is a moving experience, whether the baby is born alive or not, and every family has a tale to tell. One of the saddest times for the midwife is when she is unable to find a heartbeat and the expectant mother knows her baby will not be born alive. Supporting the mother and her family though the labour and birth and then seeing them spend time with their baby is a privilege, but also can be emotionally draining. Creating memories for them in the form of footprints, special quilted blankets or embroidered small clothing is important.

While I love my job here in NSW, one of my greatest joys has been to travel to a number of developing countries and work as a volunteer in midwifery, maternal and child health. Most recently (2012), I have been on a midwifery safari to East Africa to visit tribal groups and nomads in Uganda,

Kenya and Tanzania and learn of their birthing practices. The world of midwifery is truly amazing.

Mavis Gaff-Smith, registered nurse and midwife (Mavis has published several books including Midwives of the Black Soil Plains, No Births on Monday, Riverina Midwives *and* Midwife on a Mission.

chapter two
LOOKING BACK

Looking back across a century of nursing, much has changed but much remains the same, most notably the dedication, determination and commitment of the people who choose to work in rural and remote areas of Australia.

'My dear, if you were a horse . . .'

EAST GIPPSLAND, VICTORIA

The copper-tipped arrow shot up quickly into the darkening Gippsland sky. Behind Black Mountain the sun was sinking, leaving the creek, our little wooden house and the surrounding land in shade. My older brother Bill called out to us: 'Quick – come outside and look at this!'

My mother and I rushed out onto the verandah, leaving the baby sleeping and my sister Juliet reading inside. Bill was standing by the lucerne paddock a few hundred yards away. 'Look at this,' he said. With all his strength he drew back his bow, fitted a second arrow and released it. In a smooth, graceful arc the arrow flew upwards. As it rose higher and higher we saw the arrow-tip gleam like a spark of fire when it caught the golden light of the sun.

It was beautiful. 'Ooooh!' we cried, watching the bit of flashing gold in the sky above the shadowed land. The arrow with its brightly shining tip seemed to stay up in the sky for a long time before beginning its descent back to earth.

Just then my sister Juliet wandered out on the verandah, still reading. The arrow gracefully arced down and down and down. With stunning rapidity – *thwock!* – the arrow shot into Juliet's upper arm. With a sharp, shocked little scream, she dropped her book. By the time that I heard the book thud onto the verandah, our mother was at Juliet's side.

At times like that, back in the 1950s, in this remote part of Victoria, with no electricity and the car away through the day wherever Dad was, our mother's nursing skills came in handy. Inside, she washed and dressed the wound. It was while this was happening that my sister, looking at the layers of fat under the punctured skin on her arm, said, 'Gosh – we're just *meat*!' Apart from this existential shock, the only enduring effect was the small scar on her upper arm.

We were living on our sheep farm in Suggan Buggan (*Soog-en Boog-en*), in East Gippsland. It's a wild and beautiful place on the edge of the Snowy River, 133 kilometres north of Orbost, which is 375 kilometres east of Melbourne. It was so isolated that when we first arrived the kingfishers by the river were not scared of us. It is still isolated because, even now, not many people are keen to brave the terrifying road to the Suggan Buggan River.

We had a horse called Coco, a cow called Prim, and Bruno, the first of a series of calves. Sometimes we had pigs. There was an orchard. My mother, Roma, grew vegetables, looked after the chooks and topped up our vitamin C by making rose-hip syrup. Juliet and Bill milked the cow even though Roma said, 'Girls shouldn't milk cows before adolescence, because it will make your hands big and no man will want to marry you!'

She taught us by correspondence school. As well as this, Roma looked after anyone in the surrounding district who needed medical help. Injured or orphaned animals also received her attention. She rescued hurt birds and fed them with an eye-dropper. She rescued joeys and baby possums and fed them with a baby's bottle. When they grew a little, we children would stretch dolls' jumpers over their delicate limbs and suede-like little torsos as they looked up at us with their big trusting eyes. Two orphaned possums, Shadow and Shy, lived in an enormous cage and ate scraps from our hands.

Cattlemen drove their herds of cattle through our property every spring until the Snowy River Hydro-Electric Scheme made it impossible to get through that way. Bill Pendergast was one such regular, a tough old guy. One time, when my mother asked him how he was, he told her that he had broken his foot. She expressed concern and wanted to do what she could to mend it, insisting that he must stay until it was better.

'Oh, no,' he said, 'I'll be off after me tea, thanks. I'll just keep me boot on till it mends itself.'

After Roma died, in 2004, Juliet and I discovered two diaries from her time in the bush, scribbled in old exercise books, which she had kept in the 1950s until she needed prolonged medical attention herself, for her ailing back.

In the first diary is an account of her treating our nearest neighbour, two miles away, Viv Richardson, when he managed to spill some molten lead in his eye. Another time she fixed him up after he cut his hand while sharpening his axe.

She also treated our cousin Keith Davies' burnt feet when he ran through the ashes Bill had run through moments before. The area Bill had run through had cooled and the area Keith chose was, unaccountably, still hot. Keith's family had a dairy farm at Gelantipy, which Keith runs now.

On Wednesday, 5 May 1954, Roma wrote that my father:

. . . was working on the house, knocking down the

scaffolding when a three inch piece of board with a nail in it fell on his left hand, thumb side of wrist. Perfect puncture wound, very sore. I applied antiphlogistine poultice, after shaving it. Poor boy couldn't sleep. I did [illegible] and gave him aspirin and tea at 2 a.m. I pray to God that it doesn't give trouble. I have visions of amputation or tetanus or something.

Roma did a splendid job of looking after everyone but the responsibility clearly weighed on her sometimes: 'I gave poor Bill his H.I. of tetanus toxoid and am sitting here worried sick about a reaction. God, I hate having to give them to everyone,' she noted on 17 July 1954.

She gave the family polio injections in 1957 at Gelantipy. Some years before she died, she recalled how awful it felt to inoculate me because as she aimed the big needle at my arm, my usually placid baby face changed into an expression of disbelief, both comical and heartbreaking to see.

Roma's own health became increasingly worse as her back pain intensified. She often lay down with a hot water bottle – as hot as she could stand it – to ease the pain. Once, Juliet was filling the hot water bottle when she accidentally dropped the heavy kettle on the bench. Boiling water splashed onto the bottom half of her face. At Juliet's shriek, Roma leapt up and dealt with the resulting burn. Juliet remembers the skin peeling right off. She can't recall what Roma did, but there was no scar at all.

There are diary entries about Roma's back pain as early as 1954 when we were still living in the one-roomed hut by the river, waiting for my dad to finish building our house. On 6 May that year she wrote:

The washing seems to rob me of all my time. I stand in the
river and slosh away. I boil here and cart things down wet
and rinse them and hang them on a line by the river . . . and
how my spine screams.

When she spent a day helping our dad to put in fence posts,
she wrote, 'I love it but I pay for it.'

On 30 May 1954 she wrote, 'My back is feeling battered.'
In August of that year she saw a Dr Stafford in Bairnsdale and
then another doctor in Melbourne, and wrote:

The X-rays showed deformed vertebrae (congenital) which
slipped forward after Penelope's birth etc. He will operate
when I can get a bed – one to two months. Hell. How can
I put up with the time? Very pleased and happy that that is
my pain's cause. I was scared it would be TB of the bone,
osteomyelitis or something.

The next entry is Friday, 26 November 1954. She wrote
about having morphine four-hourly for two days after the
operation.

I couldn't have borne the pain without the injec-
tions . . . They did my back and turned me and sponged me
four hourly (sometimes six hourly and I nearly went mad
with the pain and discomfort). I couldn't sleep and had to
lie there hour after hour unable to move to lift my back one
inch off the bed . . . when the nurses came they were angels
and couldn't do enough for me.

A year later, she was staying with relatives in Sydney and seeing doctors there. She wrote in December 1955 that her cold
turned into pneumonia, with pleurisy, and that Dr Rowe was
disappointed in the state of her back and that she must rest,

and he ordered a plaster jacket for six weeks. By 13 February 1956:

Dr Rowe said he had done all he could for me and I mustn't lift anything heavy and generally take it carefully for a year or two; to wear a surgical corset and come to see him in a month's time. I am very dissatisfied at his taking no notice of the sore bones in my back and on returning here I cried and cried – I went to see Dr Ryan here and told him the whole story. He suggested an X-ray and made the appointment. I feel very depressed at my future life because the Dr said my back would go again if I didn't take care. Also he said if I had another baby the spondylolisthesis would come again and this time plaster wouldn't fix it. He said I would never be strong and never be able to nurse again, a dreadful blow to me because it is my security.

A month after her return home, her back was already weakening and aching very badly. The following day it was so bad that she stayed in bed all day and our dad had to do all the chores. He did his best, but I remember him plaiting my hair so tightly that I could hardly blink.

In July 1956, Roma found that she was pregnant. During the pregnancy she had a terrible time with her back. My brother Patrick was born in Sydney and she was away for nearly a year. The doctors thought that she wouldn't be able to walk again. After a long while, she did walk, and then after more time could do so without crutches, but she always had trouble with back pain.

Soon after July 1956 the diaries stop. There were many more visits to doctors. Roma liked her doctor's bedside manner with a dash of black humour: an oft-repeated story, always told with much hilarity, was how Dr Maxwell looked at her X-rays then looked at her, and said: 'Well, my dear, if you were a horse, I'd take you out to the paddock and shoot you.'

Not long before Roma died, she told me she didn't regret a single day of living in the bush. She said that not one child ever said that they were bored. During all that time not one of us kids ever saw a doctor. We were not exposed to the usual measles and mumps of childhood and we didn't get colds or flu. And Roma dealt with inoculations, and accidents like arrow wounds. It was a wonderful part of our childhood and although Roma was very unlucky with her back, we kids were lucky to have the experience of living in the isolated bush, and we – and the people on neighbouring properties – were lucky that our mum was a nurse.

Penelope Hanley, daughter of Roma, registered nurse

Nursing on the Wild Side

COOMA, SNOWY MOUNTAINS, NEW SOUTH WALES

I began as a nursing aide in Cooma, NSW, in the late 1950s when I was about sixteen. It was a small town then, with its claim to fame being that it was the headquarters of the Snowy Mountains hydro scheme. My stepfather, mother and two half-sisters and I lived on the outskirts of Cooma and my stepfather worked on the scheme. My mother – being a lively city girl – hated the place, missing the bright lights of the city.

It consisted of a main street with the usual shops selling food and clothing for the assortment of townspeople and out-lying farms. Then there were the local pubs. I remember two in particular, and a couple of seedy nightclubs, that were fre-quented by the migrant workers. The hospital was called a community hospital and by today's standards was very small and basic, especially considering the population explosion that the Snowy scheme brought to the area.

It was a rough, tough town. The inner perimeter was taken over by the accommodation blocks for single men and a large mess hall to feed them. There was natural enmity among the diverse nationalities, many of whom still carried grievances from their homelands. Some formed gangs and there was fierce competition among them to see who could complete tunnelling first. The local boys hated them for what they saw as their cosmopolitan sophistication and ability to attract the local females.

The hospital, apart from caring for the local and nearby farming communities, also catered for the workers who did not require intensive medical attention. Serious cases were fer-ried to Canberra or Sydney.

On certain weekends, 'the girls' from Sydney would arrive by train and be transported to the camps where, I believe, there would be lines of men waiting for their services. Gamblers would also arrive to run games. I met one young man who showed me a suitcase filled with money. These weekends usu-ally elicited fights, quite often with knives, which would result in injuries requiring hospital attention. Many of the migrant workers were young and, when in pain, wept with homesickness and loneliness.

My duties, as a dogsbody, were mainly boiling instruments, including needles and anything else that was reusable, and rolling bandages, which had been autoclaved along with the other dressings. Then there was the pan-room, dreaded by all junior nurses. I was terrified of duty on the men's ward and remember vividly the time I had the horrible embarrassment of picking up a male urinal incorrectly and spilling the contents over the ward. The men were so kind as I mopped up, as was the ward sister. I was mortified.

The women's ward had quite a few cases of dreadful bed sores – some so large you could fit your fist in them. These were generally older ladies from the outlying farms, who were bedridden for whatever reason and too proud to ask for help until their wounds needed prescriptive medical attention.

I was very young, awaiting acceptance as a probationer at a teaching hospital. Most of the girls were nursing aides like me, but I intended to go on to become a trained nurse. I only stayed in Cooma for a short time, as it was not considered a great place for a young girl to be working at the time. Still, I have many wonderful memories, such as going to a dance at Adaminaby via Jindabyne, before the area was flooded. When my time as an aide was up, I left for Brisbane and began my training as a nurse.

Beverley, retired registered nurse

Halls Creek Heroine

HALLS CREEK, KIMBERLEY REGION,
WESTERN AUSTRALIA

Mary Elizabeth Rogasch (Lil) was born in 1880 in Gawler, South Australia, and educated there. She trained at the Children's Hospital in Adelaide from 1906 to 1909. In December of that same year she received her first certificate of registration as a nurse, and in 1910 she earned a certificate in obstetrics from the Queen's Home. She also passed the necessary exams to become an Inspector of Nuisances.

Lil was a committed Christian and in 1917 was asked by the Australian Inland Mission to undertake a temporary position as a nursing sister in Oodnadatta, an isolated settlement in the north of South Australia, following the resignation of the incumbent nurse. After six months there, she travelled to Hergott Springs (Marree) to relieve Sister Clapton of the District Trained Nurses' Association for six weeks, enabling her to have a much needed break.

In 1918, Lil was given a permanent appointment with the AIM and along with an unqualified companion, Miss Mary Madigan, who was also appointed by the AIM, set off in August 1918 to face an unknown future as the first nursing sister at the newly established hospital in the remote settlement of Halls Creek, in the Kimberley region of Western Australia.

Lil and Mary travelled by train to Perth, where they met Dr Holland, who helped them buy some hospital supplies and home comforts for their accommodation. The SS *Bambra* took them from Fremantle to Wyndham, where they arrived at the end of September. From there they were to be met and escorted to Halls Creek. However, no sooner had the ship docked than an urgent message came to the Wyndham telegraph station from Halls Creek. There had been another tragic event in the settlement when Mr Ward, the storekeeper and Honorary Secretary of the new Hospital Committee, had been shot and wounded by an attacker who then fatally shot himself.

A race against time was needed as Sister Rogasch was rushed 250 miles (400 kilometres) south by a hastily requisitioned car. She treated the patient and brought him back to the doctor and hospital at Wyndham. It was a five-day round-trip over shocking terrain.

Mary Madigan sat out the five days in Wyndham. Then, once again for Lil, the two ladies headed south in an entourage of two buggies, each with four in hand, drivers, escorts and extra horses. This trip left Wyndham on 29 September 1918 and took almost two weeks. They camped out most nights or stayed at stations. The trip was very rough going through dry, sandy creek beds, timbered country and bushfires. At one stage, the ever-venturous Lil even enjoyed an exciting time driving the buggy a few miles with Tommy, the normal driver, closely monitoring the experience. On 12 October they finally arrived in Halls Creek.

The town consisted of a court house, post office, hotel, store, police station, miner's institute, and two cottages. The population was quoted as about 'twelve white people, including five children'. Visiting 'cattle-punchers' and diggers called in at times and numerous Aborigines were camped outside the township.

The hospital was the former miner's institute, which was originally built in 1898 and was made of mud brick with an iron roof. The building was completely refurbished. A new floor was laid and the walls given a fresh white wash. In her diary, Lil described it:

[Half] our building is a ward and a small room adjoining, which we use as a dressing room. Verandah all around. This half is enclosed with house canvas: you enter the door and there is our table with its homemade bookshelf lined with zinc to keep out the white ants . . . .two cyclone beds made presentable with our swag covers . . . a few cushions and a green gum bough in a rum jar constitutes our sitting, writing and rest room. Around the corner – no partition – are our dining table and chairs. Further is an annexe made cosy in the evening with a dark blue cambric table cover with a border of cretonne stitched around it. Same material covers our crockery shelves and (used) for hiding the pot box and little curtains for our window. No glass is put in small windows, a swing board affair instead. A large bowl of mignonette on the table really completes an inviting corner. We put the lounge and easy chair stovewards in the winter evenings. It is quite nice to see a tired postman resting there before he starts off for his resting place for the night . . . He had just come in from his 198 mile (318 kilometres) trek and had to go on 9 miles (14 kilometres) where there was good feed for his horses. His own bed was to be a (stock) trough filled with grass.

One room was a four-bed ward with whited walls and there was a small dispensary room. The kitchen was for both the patients and the staff. The white outside walls made the establishment look clean and inviting. A verandah ran around three sides and it was here that the patients preferred to sleep and rest.

The hospital quickly settled down and on 11 November 1918, which was in fact Peace Day, the official opening of the Halls Creek Australian Inland Mission Hospital was held. The Australian flag was raised on a pole in the hospital yard. All the settlers and some from further out attended; the national anthem was sung and speeches were made. Now the hospital could get down to do the work for which it was set up.

Initially, many people came from far and wide just to see and welcome the ladies. Patients were frequent and though some were very reticent about being cared for by a woman, they soon got over this feeling and began to savour the kindly face and tender care bestowed on them by the sister who was always in readiness for duty wherever she was needed.

Beds were occupied for up to four weeks as many of the men who came in from camps were suffering from malnutrition. Mary and Lil cooked hearty soups and meals and built the men up. A string of outpatients came in from far and wide and were treated for eye troubles; cuts and gashes that needed stitching, while sore heads and bodies were treated following drunken brawls. Broken limbs and other injuries – often as a result of a horse fall – were common. Then there were the more serious problems where the patient had to be stabilised and taken to Wyndham by buggy. On many occasions Lil would have to consult with the doctor by morse code over the telegraph line to get instructions for treatment.

She reported after the first ten months:

This no doubt seems to you a small population to need the help of a hospital, but the passing population is great and I do not think that a day goes by without someone coming in or going out . . . We have had seventeen indoor patients staying an average of twenty-eight days. When men are better, we feed them up: that makes the average stay longer than in a hospital where outside comforts are near.

When patients were admitted into the hospital ward they often preferred to be out on the verandah – they were quite used to sleeping outdoors. Lil was on duty twenty-four hours a day every day. Mary Madigan was a big comfort and help. Sometimes, when there were no patients, Fred Tuckett, who was probably the most prominent resident, sent Lil or both of them off for a walk or a horse ride while he took on the responsibility of dealing with any necessity for a few hours. Lil, however, was never too far away.

Thus Lil gave three years of dedicated work to Halls Creek. In 1920, Mary Madigan returned to Adelaide and for the next year, Lil was joined by another fully qualified sister, her own youngest sister, Sister Beatrice May Rogasch.

In 1923, Lil married Mac McCombe and they lived in Wyndham for eleven years before moving south to farm in the wheat belt. Lil died in Adelaide in 1967, aged eighty-six.

Adapted extracts from Sister Mary Elizabeth Rogasch – Halls Creek 1918–1921 *by Joan Rogasch.*

Angels of the Bush

MARANBOY, NORTHERN TERRITORY

I trained in General Nursing at the Brisbane General Hospital from 1915 to 1919 and then did my obstetric training at the Lady Bowen Hospital, also in Brisbane.

I was a member of the congregation at the Ithaca Presbyterian church. After speaking with both the Right Rev. James Gibson and the Rev. John Flynn, I was encouraged to join the Australian Inland Mission (AIM).

I asked Miss Doris Dunlop if she would accompany me to whichever centre of work the AIM sent me. We had trained together at the Brisbane General Hospital. She agreed and on 3 September 1920 we set off on an ocean steamer for Darwin, a trip that took nine days. We were the first Queensland nurses to join the AIM.

From Darwin we travelled by train and then car to Maranboy, which was to be our home for the next two years. The small tin field had a permanent population of about twenty, including five other white women. Although a number of travellers passed through Maranboy, mostly drovers and cattlemen, in all the time we were there, we did not see one white woman traveller.

The hospital was two storeys of galvanised iron set with some wire gauze for windows. It looked just like an oversized meat safe. We lived in the top floor and our patients stayed on the ground floor, which had a concrete surface. The humidity was generally about 90 per cent and the temperature between

38 and 44 degrees Celsius. We could never obtain cold water and never wore a cardigan the whole time we were there.

There was no Flying Doctor or pedal radio back then and the nearest doctor was about 320 kilometres away. We could only contact him by telegraph from the post office at the nearby tin mine.

The Aboriginal camp was not far from the hospital and on many occasions we could hear their corroborees and the persistent drumming of the didgeridoos well into the night.

Malaria was a common complaint among the few miners left in Maranboy, and they were very thankful to the AIM for the facilities for care and treatment at our hospital. Apart from the miners, our patients were people brought often long distances in to us after accidents or suffering illness.

Our stores arrived every six months by horse-drawn wagon, though we had a mail delivery every six to eight weeks. We lived on tinned foods. Fresh meat was very rare and even salted beef, carefully wrapped in a hessian bag, was a delicacy brought to us very occasionally by drovers passing by.

Soon after we arrived, some men from Mataranka brought us a puppy of mixed breed to be our protector. Named Wolf, he was a very intelligent dog and alerted us to the arrival of the postman or any travellers while they were still some way off. He would prick his ears forward and we would know to be on the lookout for visitors.

Our other friend and protector was Paddy, an Aboriginal man of about forty. He had been with the previous sister and was very proud of his position as 'hoshipal boy'. He regularly went walkabout but always came back. He would return looking quite fearsome, carrying his spears and with sticks through his nose. He called me 'Mitta Dokka'.

At three o'clock one morning, two gentlemen, Mr Francis Birtles – who, incidentally, was also the first person to drive from London to Melbourne – and Mr Roy Fry, were brought to our hospital for treatment after their car went up in flames about 130 kilometres from Maranboy. It took about three days for them to reach us and besides their third-degree burns, they were suffering from severe shock and were delirious. Sister Dunlop and I nursed them continuously for many weeks and I don't know how they recovered as their clothes were burnt right into their flesh. Eventually they were well enough to resume their journey to Darwin.

Another time, we treated an Aboriginal man who had fractured his leg. His wife, Polly, carried him to us and we put his leg in a splint. He would not remain in hospital and next morning we found him hopping around outside with the splint gone and his leg wrapped in bark. He went bush, and we understood he arrived at a station some weeks later wearing nothing but a lace blouse we had given to Polly and the crutches made for him by one of the men at the field.

One old sundowner came to us once with his foot crushed. One of his toes became gangrenous so we amputated it and insisted he stay in hospital overnight. He had never slept in sheets before but he duly recovered despite this and went on his way. A few weeks later he arrived back with his horse. It had a cancerous growth that he thought we might be able to cure. This was the only time we had to refuse a patient.

Our hospital was the centre of what little social activity there was in the district. We had a small harmonium and on Sunday evenings we sang hymns to the patients and any other callers. A party of politicians passed through once and spent the day with us. Later they sent us a gramophone and some records. This was a great joy to us but I think an even greater joy to the Aborigines who would stand around the hospital, laughing at our music until the tears rolled down their faces.

No padres or doctors came near us. There were no such people around then. Later I realised we were not far from what became known as the Rum Jungle. Little did we think there would eventually be a vast mining enterprise in the area.

Maranboy and the surrounding area was alive with long black snakes with red bellies. Sipping our afternoon tea one day, we saw Paddy become very excited. He told us there was a snake under our table! We moved and he quickly grabbed it and whirled it around his head before its head flew off. Later, we saw him proudly bear it back to his camp, where he ate it.

We had both suffered from attacks of malaria and towards the end of our time, my malarial attacks became serious indeed and I had to write and ask to be relieved of my duties. Sister Dunlop remained for the last couple of months and later married Mr Harold Giles, who became the manager of Elsey Station of *We of the Never Never* fame.

It was not until I was leaving that we were told that we had been known, for many hundreds of miles around, as Angels of the Bush. Paddy's sorrow at my departure was most touching and he wanted to come to Queensland with me to make sure I arrived safely. His actual words were, 'More better Mitta I come alonga your country.'

Adapted from the memoirs of Jean Mittelheuser (nee Herd), registered nurse, AIM

Finding Fitzroy Crossing

FITZROY CROSSING, KIMBERLEY REGION, WESTERN AUSTRALIA

It was January 1970 and I was on my way to Fitzroy Crossing in the Kimberley region of Western Australia. My dream, since I was young, was to be a nurse and as a nurse, to work with the Australian Inland Mission (AIM). The year I spent at Fitzroy Crossing was adventurous, challenging, fascinating and fulfilling. At the same time it was demanding, nerve-racking and stressful. When I look back now I realise that the rest of my nursing career was influenced by this amazing experience.

I had a short stopover in Perth for a very brief orientation that included two days of instruction on how to take and process X-rays. Two days and we were expected to be able to take readable films to diagnose fractures or congested lungs. Well, I think the only decent X-ray I took for the year was one of a sealed package containing the engagement ring my boyfriend asked his mother to choose for him! I just had to know what the ring looked like before I opened it in front of him.

The wet season was in full swing when I arrived. I flew from Derby to Fitzroy Crossing on the mail plane. I had never been on a small plane before and was just a little anxious when the pilot pulled out a book and opened it on his knees as he took off. I wondered if he needed the instructions in order to fly the plane. However, we arrived safely and the heat hit me like a wall as I stepped out onto the airstrip. The temperature was over 43 degrees Celsius for the first two weeks I was there. I felt like a wrung-out rag as I tried to take in all the advice I was given by the current staff.

The hospital was staffed by three nurses, with another nurse going out to the stations running 'field clinics'. We would look after inpatients, outpatients and cooking on a weekly basis. The outpatient nurse would do any night work that was necessary. I have never worked anywhere else where all the staff went to bed at night and the patients would come and get us if we were needed. This was, of course, as long as there was no-one ill enough to need constant care.

Cooking for the staff, any visitors and the occasional white patient was a challenge. We were inexperienced cooks as well as inexperienced nurses. Our Aboriginal staff cooked for the rest of the patients in their own style on a camp fire. Our meat was brought in from one of the stations usually on the back of a truck covered with gum leaves. The sight of a full leg of beef being dumped on the table was a bit daunting. I had no idea of the different cuts of meat, so it was all cut into sections and frozen. None of us knew anything about freezing food and we just placed the meat onto trays and it was stored in the freezer uncovered! When we needed meat we partly thawed it, cut off enough for the meal and then refroze the rest. No wonder the health inspector shook his head in despair.

Our patients were mostly Aboriginal. Many of the children suffered from severe gastroenteritis or respiratory infections. An episode of gastro could trigger a downward spiral and they became extremely sick very quickly. The level of dehydration determined when the plane would be sent out so that the child could be evacuated to the Derby hospital. Although we consulted with the doctors, we were their eyes and ears so it was up to us to do an accurate assessment.

Our doctors were from the Royal Flying Doctor Service (RFDS). They would come out once a week or fortnight to run a clinic. In between clinics we could consult with the doctors via the two-way radio. There was an open medical session each morning. This meant you were describing symptoms to the doctor knowing that dozens of people may be listening in too. To save embarrassment we soon learnt to fully assess the patient before we went on air. When we had an emergency and felt we needed a patient evacuated, we could ring the RFDS at the Derby hospital and get direct advice. If it was to be a night flight, the medical superintendent would come out on the plane himself. He would ask us, 'Is it was worth risking my life?' What a dilemma it was to be confident enough in your assessment to say 'yes'.

A night flight meant lighting the airstrip. This would mean we would have to locate the local police officers and ask them to light the flares. When we heard the plane overhead we would load the patient into the back of the hospital ute and drive out to meet it. It was a small town and a night flight gave the locals a bit of excitement. We, however, just hoped we had made the right decision.

Knowledge of things mechanical would have been helpful but I had none. As well as the hospital ute to maintain, we had a generator for power and a diesel pump for our water. I became stressed every time I had to crank the pump to turn it on. We turned the generator off during the day after the chores were done and also at night. One night I came back to the nurses' quarters, after turning off the generator, and noticed a movement across the track. I called for one of the other girls to bring a torch and there in front of me was a huge king brown snake! We kept long-handled shovels around the buildings so we grabbed one each and with great trepidation we killed the snake. I was shaking like a leaf.

In the wards we had low metal stretchers with a mattress, sheet, pillow and a grey blanket. However, at night you would find the patients sleeping on the floor huddled around a hurricane lamp. During the day they would sit out in the garden under the trees. We would have to go out and find them to give medications or do dressings. It was such a contrast to our big sterile hospitals down south.

A piece of equipment that caused much hilarity and anxiety was our gas 'autoclave'. It worked like a pressure cooker. We would place a wrapped bundle of linen and instruments in it, clamp down the lid and light the gas. Steam hissed out a valve at the top and we had to adjust a lever to control the pressure. The bundle was wet when we took it out and we had to place it in the sun in order to dry the linen. I'm glad our modern-day 'infection control' nurses were not there to see it!

The annual race meeting and rodeo gave us all some entertainment. Although we had to look after any patients and deal with any injuries, we still had time to see a good bit of the action. The station people for miles around would attend so it was a real social occasion. The Race Ball was a highlight and I remember sewing a special dress for the night. We were in great demand as dance partners as there were more men than women in the area.

So many memories come back to me. We swam at beautiful Brooking Gorge, had dust storms that rolled in across the paddocks and left behind a terrible mess to clean up and experienced tropical storms that provided spectacular sound and light shows. We lived beside the mighty Fitzroy River and were awed by the sight of it in flood.

We were young nurses with limited experience volunteering to do a job that stretched our capabilities. It was a privilege to work with the people of the area, both black and white. We did not realise it at the time but we were part of history and are proud of the work we did.

Beryl Scott, retired registered nurse

Well Done, Bush Nurses
WARBURTON, FAR EASTERN
WESTERN AUSTRALIA

Nursing in an isolated community is certainly different. There were four of us, all double certificate registered nurses from Queensland, New South Wales and Western Australia. We met in Perth to do some preliminary training in nursing protocol and basic vehicle maintenance. We also enjoyed our last taste of shops, dining out and bright city lights.

Somewhere on the journey to Warburton, out in the desert about 1500 kilometres north-east of Perth, we each recognised the enormity of the task ahead. However, our enthusiasm for this adventure never waned. We hardly knew each other and now we were going to be living and working closely together for the next year or so, in a place we didn't know, with people who spoke languages we didn't understand. It was a challenge that called for patience, respect, good listening skills, friendliness and a good sense of humour.

We learnt a lot about each other on the long drive out to Warburton, along rough, sandy roads towing a large caravan that was to be our sleeping quarters until the nurses' home was built. Dust, flies, taking our turn at driving and cooking, adjusting to the heat and never-ending landscape were all part of this team building process. My three companions were good women, great nurses, reliable under pressure, and I learnt much from them in the time we spent at Warburton.

A new hospital and nurses' quarters was to be built at Warburton. In the meantime, the old hospital was our home and workplace, though we continued to sleep out in the caravan. Other staff at Warburton included school teachers, community welfare department workers, government liaison workers, office staff (for processing pensions, mail, telegrams, and meteorological info four times daily, etc.), a maintenance man and some missionary linguists. The Aboriginal community consisted of several tribes who mostly lived in humpies, though some lived in stone houses. There was a substantial dirt airstrip, a community store and a fuel facility.

Nursing care was available twenty-four hours a day, seven days a week. We held clinics every morning and evening and we delivered babies and kept patients in hospital overnight when necessary. One of our priorities was to establish a community nursing program. Even though we could usually find someone to interpret when we needed to, we needed to learn the languages, so we took lessons with the missionary linguists. These were interesting and helpful, though we could only have lessons at night when we were probably not at our best for learning.

Each morning, we used the radio schedule with the RFDS in Kalgoorlie to consult with doctors, knowing that they were available any time for emergencies as well. Doctors visited on a regular basis for clinics, a highlight for us professionally and socially. The visits ensured good patient care and entertainment for the whole community. Most patients, no matter how sick, didn't want to leave their country and people to go to the unknown; however, emergency air transport to hospital in Kalgoorlie was always available, when required.

I remember my very first clinic. The noise of people yelling to each other outside, mothers trying to quiet crying children inside and lots of people in queues waiting their turn, the smells, noise, confusion and laughter were so different from hospitals I had worked at previously. One little boy had a dead bird in his hand and a big smile on his face. He kept twisting the bird's neck and could hardly wait to get out to a fire to cook it! It was amazing how quickly one felt at home in all of this. The Aboriginal kids loved to colour in, so we had lots of kids on the verandah at the weekend to colour in the drawings we had prepared. It was great to hear their chatter.

Inter-tribal fighting was a problem. Some fights lasted for hours with lots of yelling, men with spears, women wailing and people running back and forth. We learnt to treat spear wounds, suture machete cuts and tend cut heads from where women had been hitting themselves on the heads with stones.

There was a power plant generating electricity during the day. We all learnt patience while treating the paraffin fridge with lots of tender loving care. The telephone system was the old party line around the town area, with the phone having separate mouth and ear pieces and the wind-up handle. Communication with the outside world was done by mail or telegram. Our donkey (hot water system) worked really well, especially when we remembered to light it and keep the fire going! Clearing blocked pipes and drains was all part of the romance of working in the bush though, mostly, we could find someone to help us out.

A mouse plague seemed to last for months; I've never seen so many mice in all sorts of places. While eating a meal you could hear them running over the dishes on the sink. In bed, the mice would run over you, stopping for a chew on your hair. We had traps to catch up to four mice at a time, and you'd hardly have walked away when the trap was full and ready to be emptied. Many a scream was heard at night while doing rounds by candlelight, as a nurse stepped on an unsuspecting mouse or it jumped out in front of her on a work bench.

There also seemed to be nearly as many lean and scruffy-looking dogs. I often saw dogs sneaking a lick or two of flour while it was being mixed in the bowl ready to make a damper. Rubbish bins were 44-gallon drums suspended between two posts, which made them easy to empty. Many clever dogs would climb into these bins for a free feed. The drums rocked back and forth while the dog was inside. Meanwhile, some of the children, armed with their slingshots of tyre rubber and stones, would find the swinging, squeaking bins and wait in readiness to shoot at the dogs as they climbed out. The dogs were safe most of the time and it provided lots of entertainment for these developing little hunters.

Church was held on Sunday mornings after clinic, out in the dirt under two large trees. Men and women sat separately and the dogs sat around the outside of the women and children. Often we nurses were late to this gathering and had to work our way through the dogs to a spot in the dirt. Dogs and children went off playing during church but in a place where mothers could watch them. Church was all in language delivered by the Aboriginal pastor. We recognised lots of the songs by their tune, not the words. It was good to sit with people in church, taking time to worship God, and feeling the sense of God's presence with us out in the middle of Australia.

When communion was held the pastor pointed to another place and gave the hand sign of drinking. So we went too. Sitting in a circle in the dirt, the bread was a small damper which the pastor took and broke in half and walked around giving each of us a pick at it. The wine was cold, sweet, black tea in a well-used billycan. Very tricky to put the billy to your mouth and take a sip without estimating badly and spilling it down your front, leaving little for the rest of the group.

Because of the isolation, regular trips to town were non-existent so short holidays, out of the community, visiting tourist sites some kilometres away were taken in turn by the staff. These were a necessary part of keeping our sanity and freshness to our work in the bush. On weekends, there would be a get-together, with other white staffers at someone's house, for meals, games or singsongs and sharing experiences. These were good fun nights.

A Presbyterian pastor, who was a talented bagpipes player, visited our community once. It was unique to hear him playing his bagpipes as he walked round the streets of the town area, dressed in his kilt, with children following and mimicking him and laughing with the sheer exhilaration of this novelty. I have never heard the bagpipes sound so good.

There was always letter writing to friends and family back home, keeping up with correspondence, listening to music, reading and generally sharing stories and other mayhem in the nurses' quarters. We'd sometimes visit one or other of the Aboriginal camps, just sitting and talking together with the women and sharing stories. It was an amazing way of learning from each other and building friendships. The power plant engine needed to be turned off at night, so walks in the cool quiet of the night to the pump shed were a welcome break from routine. The stars seemed so close and brilliant, in the vast expanse of the night sky, in the centre of Australia.

Finding your place in the team and contributing consistently through the good and the bad is essentially the backbone of a good unit. We didn't always get it right – we are human after all – but respecting each other and having the fortitude to politely confront issues before they got out of hand created a better working atmosphere. My team mates were good at this.

Living in an isolated place, making the most of the life you had, was a satisfying lesson to absorb. We learnt to appreciate the beauty of the desert, its colours, vastness, ruggedness, amazing big skies, wildflowers and wildlife. Shivering in its cold, sweltering in its heat, dealing with the flies, working together, providing good-quality health care without hesitation, we were indeed bush nurses.

Marilyn Watson, registered nurse and midwife

Cut Loose

DERBY, NORTHERN WESTERN AUSTRALIA

While staying in Derby, I met a nurse called Maisie who was having her orientation before taking up the position of the first community nurse at Halls Creek. Maisie was from Victoria and quite a bit older than most of the nurses there. I remember thinking at the time that she seemed ill-equipped for the task ahead of her, as she had never been off a bitumen road before.

I later asked Maisie what preparation she'd had for this job. None! Had she had any experience driving a 4WD vehicle on dirt roads? None! Did she have any mechanical knowledge? None! Could she change a tyre if it had a puncture? Yes, her brother had a Land Rover just like the one she drove and he had shown her how. He had demonstrated it all very fast so she made him do it again step by step while she wrote it all down on a card that she kept in her glove box. At the time, she told me she hadn't had to use it.

It amazed me that the health department could send a person to travel those roads with no experience and no training to deal with whatever she might meet.

I have since worked for the health department and I am not so amazed.

Adapted from 'The Four Wheel Drive' by Liz Robson, Louisa Downs Station, 1969–1971, courtesy of the Kimberley Nurses History Group publication, Boughsheds, Boabs and Bandages: Stories of Nursing in the Kimberley

Forever a Nurse

NORTHERN TERRITORY AND
WESTERN AUSTRALIA

After doing her training in Perth, my mum, Midge Morrison (now aged eighty-four), went off to Tennant Creek in the Northern Territory to 'nurse the world'. She met my father there and wherever he gained employment, either in a town or managing a station, the employer got Mum for free as she would start a clinic for the place, including the Aboriginal camps. She'd have clinic evenings, baby days, immunisation days and, of course, doctor's day when the Doc would fly in after us kids got the goats and old Bluey, the horse, off the airstrip.

One time, in 1968, at Mainoru, we were awakened by a couple of Aborigines who'd been brought up to the homestead: a sick old woman and an ill two-year-old child who had come in from the bush way north in Arnhem Land. We were the first white people they had ever seen.

Mum was clinic sister in Pine Creek for many years, operating out of an old silver bullet caravan parked at the back of the police station. This wasn't always the best place to be as some of the Aborigines wouldn't seek her medical help in case the policeman saw them and locked them up on some outstanding warrant.

From Pine Creek, she ran a highway beat from Adelaide River all the way down to Katherine. As there was no ambulance at Pine Creek, if any patients needed transferring to either of these places, she would simply take them in her Mini Moke and flag the ambos down on the road, meeting them halfway.

One time, a road train with three trailers hauling fuel rolled and when Mum got to the scene of the accident, the driver was sitting up against a tree. When Mum asked him what happened, he said he'd been checking out the inside of his eyelids! Another time she thought a severely bashed woman had her brains exposed, but it turned out to be fire ash placed on the head wound to stem the bleeding.

In the early 1970s, Mum went to Onslow in Western Australia as the community health nurse and had a large beat there servicing pastoral properties and, of course, the local Aboriginal community. One time, a cyclone was imminent and I took a call at home from the local copper who asked where Mum was, as everyone was supposed to be safe and sound at home. By this time, the winds were getting pretty strong and we were on red alert. They found Mum down the camp hammering sheets of tin with 3-inch nails trying to help make the camp safer.

Five years ago I was residing in Exmouth and got talking to a young man whose name I recognised. He had been a child on a station that was part of Mum's Onslow run. I told him that Mum was the clinic sister and this (by now thirty-year-old) man's eyes widened and he asked, 'Sister Morrison?' with horror. He went on to tell me that as soon as Mum drove in to the station, he and his brothers would run for the sand dunes. Apparently, after Mum had had her chat and a cuppa with the boys' mother, their mother would call to them to come and say goodbye to my mum. They would obediently do so and then mum and their mum would grab them and they'd receive their next immunisations!

Mum went south to Mandurah for a few years and worked in mainstream hospital emergency rooms and the like, but found it very stifling with the hierarchy and protocols. Soon she found herself over in Queensland doing relief nursing at various Aboriginal communities.

Throughout the year, she would beg other nurses for their old uniforms, which she'd take to New Guinea each Christmas period to relieve the Salvation Army bush nurses at remote village outposts near Kainantu in the Highlands. The villagers had her trekking over mountains for two days to reach and treat patients. She even performed an emergency tracheotomy up there. She would return to Australia with a completely empty suitcase.

I recall an old drunk, who went through a plate glass window and refused to go to hospital. He would only see Mum, who proceeded to sew him up with 150-plus stitches.

The people of Pine Creek and Onslow all have very fond memories and a great respect for my mother.

She had six children and mostly brought us up singly, as things were often hard at home with my father (who had war neurosis). For me, she's my mum, but for her, being a nurse has always been *who* she really was.

Fiona Gorman, daughter of Midge Morrison, retired registered nurse

The Way It Was

SOUTH AUSTRALIA

I commenced my training in 1960 at the Adelaide Children's Hospital and I am still working part-time. In those days if you got married you automatically had to resign. The same if you became pregnant. If you wanted to have a profession, earn money and be independent of your parents, you abstained from sex as the best policy. Contraception came in a bit later. We all had to live in the nurses' home and did we have some fun. The ways we found to get in and out of the home after hours were ingenious.

I looked at our exam paper the other day. One question was how to do a nasal toilet. That was in 1963. Students now would laugh at that. They are much better equipped with knowledge on all subjects, but they still can't arrange the pillows for comfort like we were taught or change a dirty bed without it going everywhere. The Sisters in Charge were very conscious of their laundry bill.

I can remember one night, while working at a country hospital, we had to take a corpse to the morgue across the car park. It was dark and raining, we were hurrying and we hit a pothole. The body ended upon the ground so I now know what a 'dead weight' means.

Nursing has been so good to me over the last forty-eight years.

Christina Mowbray, retired registered nurse

Adventure in Andamooka

ANDAMOOKA, SOUTH AUSTRALIA

In 1965, my husband and I took our two-year-old son to live in Andamooka to try our luck on the opal fields. The Australian Inland Mission had recently established a hospital there and as I have general and midwifery certificates, I made myself known to the staff. Over the next few years the sisters occasionally called on me for help and to relieve when they went on leave.

When my husband was killed in a mining accident in 1973, there happened to be a changeover of staff at the hospital, so I asked Mr Doug Lyons and Rev. Max Griffiths if they would consider me for the position. They agreed and decided that instead of there being two staff members it would be just me, thus leaving the second bedroom for my two children.

The work was certainly challenging and very well worth doing. It helped that people knew me and could talk to me. It was very satisfying to me that, while at the hospital, I ran two courses of St John's First Aid, with everyone graduating after taking their exams with examiners from Woomera.

The Flying Doctors flew up from Port Augusta and held a clinic once a fortnight, and were always ready with advice over the two-way radio phone. To evacuate sick and injured to Port Augusta, the retrieval plane had to land on a salt pan a few kilometres away. I was an ambulance driver as well as attending nurse. If it was dark we set battery lamps out: red at both ends and green at the sides. Thank goodness for the excellent RFDS pilots.

For the duration of the wet season, sometimes we had to survive without the RFDS clinic runs. The longest time we had to endure was six weeks. During this time, one morning at breakfast a man arrived to tell me his wife had been in labour since midnight. It was to be her second caesarean and she should have been sitting safely in Port Augusta at this time. In fact, she had been until her husband became lonely and drove down and brought her home!

After a moment of panic, I phoned Dr Sadler in Port Augusta. He got in touch with Woomera Weapons Research Establishment and they, thankfully, sent a helicopter to pick up my mother-to-be, who was met in Woomera by the RFDS, who in turn got her safely to the appropriate delivery room.

Around the same time, because of the flood waters, a couple of Andamooka residents informed me they had run out of their medications. The doctors were holding a clinic in Coober Pedy that day so, ever resourceful, they bought a plastic doll and stuffed it with the required pills. The pilots fashioned a parachute from an old sheet and, as they flew past on their way home, they parachuted the doll down to me.

My advice to all nurses thinking about remote area nursing? If you are prepared to treat chooks with vitamin K injections because of alleged poisoning by neighbours with rat poison; little dogs in difficulty in labour; bigger dogs suffering after dog fights with eyes hanging out; and then, of course, all your human patients, then go for it! You will love it.

Sister Fay Tilmouth, retired registered nurse

Basking in Bamaga
BAMAGA, FAR NORTH QUEENSLAND

I was brought up as a country girl and always wanted to be a nurse. The love of the bush never leaves, so after graduating in 1970 (General and Midwifery) it was only natural that my career would eventually move from busy capital cities to rural and remote areas, especially after seeing the monument to Flynn of the Inland and hearing the story on my earlier travels.

By the early nineties, I was single again with a grown-up son, so decided to travel around Australia. After visiting Cape York with a friend I was given the opportunity to go back and work at the hospital in Bamaga, which is situated about 10 kilometres from the tip of Cape York. The population there consists mainly of Torres Strait Islanders and Aboriginals and we worked under the umbrellas of Thursday Island and Cairns Base hospitals.

Most transfers were sent by helicopter to TI (Thursday Island), about a ten-minute flight. My first important lessons were to gauge which way the wind was blowing as you want to land into the wind; not have the wind pushing you from behind; and how to light and position the flares on the landing pad. Most importantly, you had to get any dogs or horses off the pad. The locals up there were not fussed about flying, but quite happy to be in a tinny in those rough oceans to the north where distance was measured in jerry cans of fuel needed for that particular trip. Any sort of flying was avoided if possible.

The locals do have a wonderfully relaxed attitude towards life so that times and dates meant nothing. This was quite frustrating for me at first, but I soon learnt that you had to go with the flow. We always worked with a local enrolled nurse (EN). Often it was only the two of you on duty with a doctor on call. The ENs had very basic training but were worth their weight in gold when it came to keeping you safe and giving you access to clients who would call in. Because family names were handed down it was essential to get the correct file. For instance, I thought I was being very smart one day and collected a file I required, only to have everyone burst into laughter when the file was for an old lady and the client I had in front of me was her granddaughter who was obviously expecting a baby. I left the file finding to the professionals after that, and date of birth took on a whole new meaning.

Child rearing was done by the whole community so you often saw children out and about with different families. Everyone was related in some way or another so criticism was best avoided. Once you gained the confidence of the EN, you gained the confidence of the community. However, this did not happen overnight.

They loved their food and took ages preparing lunch at work. Then they sat down and talked and ate in a relaxed manner. I soon realised this time could be made into fun food learning sessions and the exchanging of recipes. So much for the usual life of the nurse who eats her food on the run, especially in the big city hospital.

They loved the outdoors, so our antenatal clinics left the confines of four walls and were held under shady trees in local parks or in someone's backyard.

One never went into the house unless invited. I thought I was going up there to teach them but in reality they taught me. I learnt to stop and smell the roses. I learnt to listen and to hear. I learnt to look and to see. I learnt to feel and see both sides of the story. And I learnt to draw on past experiences and use my gut feeling when nothing was obvious at the time.

We sent our clients off to have their babies in TI and they usually stayed there unless, of course, there was a football match on in town. Then they would come back, by tinnie, hopefully getting back to TI in time for the birth.

Often you are working with no access to machines or the latest of technology. I remember walking into the emergency birthing suite and asking where the CTG (cardiotocography) machine was. Is the latest technology even the answer when you can't follow through? Better to concentrate on basics and what you can do in the present situation.

We as 'whites' are so hung up about paper work and time restraints that it's slowly choking us. These people were not early risers and our times were adjusted accordingly. I remember a new rule that came out that all staff must wear enclosed shoes. Usually, if shoes were worn at all, it was sandals and thongs. My faithful EN had worn her new shoes for quite a few days when she finally told me, 'No more shoes.' She promptly took them off and sat down. The shoes landed on the floor and out fell pieces of squashed paper. Never having had new shoes before, she had no idea that the usual stuffed paper in the shoes had to be removed.

I learnt tolerance and patience and I also learnt to question the way of the white fellow. I know we are not always right and we have much to learn. Sometimes we never ask what they want; we think we know and we get frustrated and annoyed when they don't want to do things our way.

Now I have retired after forty-six years of nursing but when I look back on my amazing career, it's the years I spent in rural and remote that will always mean the most. I could never see my career going back into a hospital situation after going rural/remote. Not only do you see parts of our amazing country that you would never see otherwise, but the exchange of ideas, food, culture, traditions and the back to basics of nursing is so refreshing and often there is not a computer in sight. It really does make you feel like a real nurse.

Lyle Barter, registered nurse (remote area nurse)

The Nearest Nurse

CHANNEL COUNTRY,
FAR SOUTH-WEST QUEENSLAND

Living in a remote community where there is no medical help at all ensures that anyone who has been in the nursing profession is called upon to assist, advise, and perform miracles. In the days when phones were unreliable and the RFDS was still several hours away, the medical problems were expected to be handled by the nearest nurse. Never mind that that particular nurse had never been trained to work without a doctor close by, or other mentors, and also that there was no equipment except maybe a thermometer, a watch and the nurse's hands. Luckily most communities and rural stations had the good old RFDS medical box.

These boxes contained medicines in bottles or boxes with numbers on them to identify the product or medication. There were bandages with numbers, eye droppers, eye glasses (for washing out the eye), medicine glasses, rubber tubing for tourniquets, thermometers (usually useless because of the heat), syringes and needles, and other miscellaneous first-aid equipment.

The medications were only to be given with the doctor's permission, except in emergency. In the early days before expiry dates, some of these products were unusable because they were affected by the heat and there was no airconditioning back then. These days the boxes are checked regularly and replaced when expired. Some of the medications are kept under refrigeration.

Mothers with babies and young children were happy to have someone to ask for advice on problems affecting their children, such as colds, coughs, vomiting and diarrhoea, constipation and many other things, and to have that person ring the doctor on their behalf, as most of them were in awe of doctors at that time and worried about saying the wrong thing, or just not knowing what to say. I think people were always reassured by having someone to take control in situations where they had no experience.

Wounds and sutures were fairly common, and suture materials were given to most of us by colleagues. Instruments were boiled in a saucepan on the stove (in rain water so they wouldn't be corroded by bore water) and the operation was generally performed on the dining table. It was usually necessary to have a torch holder assist. This often sorted out the 'gung-ho' from the helpful. It wasn't unusual to have the torch holder end up on the floor! I found that some of my children, and in particular one grandchild, were the most reliable for this job if they were around. My husband usually entertained the relatives with cups of tea and stories while the job was being done. At times it was required to keep the patient close by for observation and this required giving them a bed. Sometimes it was necessary to do regular wound dressings or check on people who had been unwell, so this required home visits.

There were some very distressing events, often involving a death. Sometimes it was necessary to organise for a deceased person to be taken to a morgue, usually by the policeman, or to arrange for a funeral. This was made harder by the fact that the person and relatives were usually well known in the community.

Gymkhanas, rodeos and other horse sports were not my favourite times. There were usually some accidents. In fact, the very first gymkhana I attended, when I didn't really know anyone well, a young rider broke his leg and I was called on to help. All we could do was get a door to place him on and get him to the RFDS plane. That was many years ago and things are a lot different now in terms of treatment and retrieval.

There were also, of course, happy events and some very humorous things that happened. There was a John Wayne episode one day, when a man brought his son to me saying he was shot! Turns out the two young brothers had a gun and one accidently (we think!) shot the other in the upper arm. It was a small shotgun and dad wanted the pellets removed. His advice to me was to 'give him some whisky and a hot knife'! However, I sent him up to Jundah hospital to have it sorted, and it was decided to leave the pellets as they were not harming anything.

Anne Kidd, retired registered nurse

Managing the Mountain
MANGROVE MOUNTAIN,
CENTRAL NEW SOUTH WALES

When I asked the Bush Nursing Association (BNA), in 1970, if I could to go to Mangrove Mountain, an isolated spot in from the central NSW coast, they practically handed it to me on a platter. The Bush Nursing Centre had been closed for eight months. In preparation for going up, the head office sent me to St Vincent's where I learnt to suture, pick bits out of eyes and look at anything that came in as a casualty. There was a policy manual there, which I was asked to read.

The day I travelled up there I had a flat tyre, locked myself out, finally got in, lit a fire and smoked myself out. This was fun! The CWA ladies had cleaned the place out, scrubbing it from top to bottom. Next morning, I woke to find mice had danced all through the draws and cupboards. That became a daily cleaning exercise until a young man named Ross found a floorboard missing in a cupboard. I was so thankful because after three weeks I was ready to leave.

I was 'on call' 24/7 but I could have two days off as deemed by the committee of locals from the mountain and surrounding districts. My hours off were from 8 a.m. to 10 p.m. on Tuesdays and Thursdays. The committee was very conscious of the community needs and it was they who raised the funds to pay me – of course, they funded that in part with the takings from the clinic. A visit to the clinic cost $1.20 and a home visit was $2.50. Patients paid mileage and for any medication I gave them; everything was carefully recorded. As the community was responsible for paying me there were a few times the wage could not be met but I never went without; I was kept very well with lots of vegetables, eggs, milk and chickens (both prepared and alive).

No two days were the same and I spent most of my time at the clinic unless called out. Then I left a sign on the clinic door saying either 'car accident' or 'home visit'. I worked one late night a week, from 5 p.m. to 8 p.m. – this was good for mothers as they could nip up with their children for their vaccines.

Every day, there were the usual fractures, cuts, bites and stings. People turned up with odd spiders in bottles or with tourniquets applied, sometimes in the wrong place. I had to know how to recognise them quickly so I didn't make a mistake, so I went off to the Reptile Park at Gosford where I bought books and asked lots of questions. I never held any of the antivenoms in my clinic as I was not considered far enough from Gosford hospital.

Farm accidents were many and varied. Suturing was a big part of my day. I dressed burns and the occasional shotgun wound. One day, I had a patient with a fractured leg, plaster intact, who rode in on horseback for me to check the plaster and the circulation in his toes. At least once a year I delivered an early baby, one of them right on my doorstep.

I attended a lot of accidents on the Pacific Highway and on the main road through to Newcastle. Long weekends were the worst; I could be out for hours. It was hardly worth my time undressing so I used to just lie on my bed and if I slept, well and good, otherwise I was up and away with a sign on the car, extra torches and my special bag and oxygen. The ambulance officers and police were very helpful to me and gave me every assistance in some rather sticky situations.

We had a large population of Greeks and Italians and smaller groups of Maltese and Turkish people. This meant I sometimes needed an interpreter. I often had to use younger members of the family but I refused to learn any of their languages and spoke English at all times.

On Sundays, I taught at the local Sunday school and throughout the years I taught first aid to the Brownies, Girl Guides and Scouts. Folk knew my times at the Centre and always knew where I was out of hours so they would just find me when they needed me. I always carried everything with me in my car in case of an accident. I became a member of the CWA, who were great supporters of the Bush Nursing Centre.

Every year, I looked forward to going down to Sydney with the president of the committee to attend the AGM of the BNA. I enjoyed comparing notes with the other bush nurses who were able to get there.

When the BNA finished in Mangrove Mountain in 1975, I stayed on for another seventeen and a half years as the community nurse. It was an interesting and challenging position and I met some very odd characters but they were all part of the mix. Lots of people looked out for me and offered help.

I was very surprised and honoured to be awarded an MBE. The citation read, 'For services to nursing and the community since 1970. Miss Eleanor Boxsell has been the bush nurse at Mangrove Mountain, an isolated area on the Central Coast of NSW, and has been almost the sole source of continuous medical care to the scattered community. She has displayed outstanding devotion to duty.'

I didn't know anyone in the outside world even knew what I was doing.

Eleanor Boxsell, MBE, retired registered nurse, midwife, child health nurse

Once a Nurse, Always a Nurse

CHARLEVILLE, SOUTH-WEST QUEENSLAND

I came to Australia for a year in the early '70s, working in Perth, Sydney and for a short stint at the Springsure Hospital in central Queensland because I wanted to visit the outback. I went back to England, but really, there were much better opportunities out here so I returned to Sydney in 1974.

I met my future husband Peter and moved to Charleville Hospital to work until we married and moved to 'Patricia Park', at Adavale, in far south-west Queensland. I ran the Adavale Clinic for many years and relieved the matron at the

Quilpie Hospital as required. I was the sole nurse at Adavale but in England I'd had a very comprehensive training at the Queen Elizabeth Hospital in Birmingham and later worked as a midwife and paediatric nurse, so I had experienced a wide variety of challenges and acquired broad range of skills. I was isolated but unafraid.

Later on, we moved to another property closer to Charleville although still 80 kilometres from town, much of this being dirt road. I worked as Director of Nursing for the Blue Nursing Service in Charleville prior to being the Director of Nursing at the Charleville Base Hospital for some years, and participated in various health forums and committees because the health and wellbeing of the community has always interested me.

In thirty-seven years working as a registered nurse in south-west Queensland, I have seen a lot of changes in rural and remote health, the most notable being the introduction of specialist fields in medicine. Generally, GPs are no longer required to provide specialist services like obstetrics, anaesthetics and surgery. Back in those days, the local GP could deliver a baby, whip out an appendix or deliver an anaesthetic for someone else in theatre. The hospitals were much busier because the wards were often full of kids with gastro and adults with stomach ulcers. Treatments are so much better now so we don't see that so much any more.

Of course, back then, there were more GPs and many country hospitals were training venues for registered and enrolled nurses, so there was a culture of learning that was attractive to staff. A local lass could train at a large country hospital, go to a regional or city hospital for a block of lectures and practical experience and return each year with new skills and more confidence. In Charleville, we had several private doctors attending the Base Hospital, including Louis Ariotti, who was a very resourceful and successful surgeon and teacher.

Nowadays, you mostly have to go to the city for those services and much less is being done in country hospitals, although there are visiting specialists in some larger rural hospitals. The closure of many maternity wards has made a significant difference to hospital numbers and also to the health and wellbeing of young parents. It's expensive to travel away for regular visits to an obstetrician and to have to be away from home for the delivery.

On the other hand, these days there are more allied health professionals. We have wonderful domiciliary nursing services in the country and things like palliative care, respite for carers, meals on wheels and so on and the ongoing use of technology, in particular telemedicine, should enable more consultations for patients and health professionals. People just need to be taught how to access things for themselves.

I've retired, more or less. I'm still vitally interested in rural and remote health though, so I've gone back to study in the field of dementia. It's a growing challenge and I'd like to continue contributing, to say nothing of keeping my own brain busy and healthy. It seems a very appropriate choice at my age!

Maggie Wade, registered nurse, midwife, paediatric nurse

City Girl

MORVEN, SOUTH-WEST QUEENSLAND

I came out, from Brisbane to south-west Queensland, fourteen years ago when my children were in their late teens and twenties. The family joke is that Mum left home first! I was single and looking to travel but, in the end, I didn't get very far. I was supposed to go to Injune, but I got a phone call the night before I was to travel telling me that Injune had cancelled and asking could I go to Augathella instead. I had never even heard of it and had to get the map out to find out where it was.

After working in the top echelons as a colorectal nurse in Brisbane, I found myself floundering. I suffered many a terrifying moment, in those early months in Augathella, as I struggled to become multiskilled. To my horror, the doctor wasn't even on the premises 24/7. It didn't matter that he was just 50 metres away in his house; I was used to having a doctor right there, at my beck and call. The staff were stand-offish at first as, I now know, is the way of the bush. You have to prove yourself before you're accepted. Despite that, it was an absolute pleasure to work with the enrolled nurses at Augathella. Enrolled nurses in the bush are the stable base of most hospitals and these were local girls who had experience I only dreamt of. I quickly understood that I needed to learn from them so I asked a million questions. I do think they often tired of me and thought me a bit of a strange one.

My first experience with the bush telegraph was on a particularly cold morning when I went walking expecting to warm up enough not to require a jumper. However, it was so cold I shivered all the way. When I got back to the hospital, I called in to have morning tea with the girls and they all laughed because they'd already been told via the bush telegraph that I was silly enough to go down town without a coat. For a city girl it was very confronting to think I was being watched every step of the way. Now, many years later, I embrace that watching, caring nature of bush people; to belong and to be cared about.

I learnt a myriad of things in Augathella; I looked in kids' ears, sutured wounds, did home visits to the elderly – all fascinating stuff and skills I'd never used in the city. My experience base expanded and I moved on to Charleville, a much bigger town and a larger hospital. I worked on what was called the General Ward. Well, wasn't that an understatement! One moment you'd be looking after an elderly person, the next somebody with a mental health issue, and then somebody having a heart attack would present.

Again, I felt my skills were lacking. I watched and learnt. The staff were amazing and I worked in awe of them. One day, at a social event, I got talking to the District Manager about my doubts in myself despite having been so in command of my practice in Brisbane. He suggested that I make a plan and upskill.

I pondered that for a long time until, one day, a lady had a nasty haemorrhage after having a baby. There wasn't always a midwife on shift after a delivery and as I was the most senior registered nurse on duty, it was me who had to deal with it. Happily, her outcome was good but it was the catalyst I needed to begin a new 'upskilling' journey.

I had always admired the mystical nurses who worked by themselves in the bush, attending to everything in their communities. I completed my Rural and Isolated Practice (RIPRN) course and Midwifery. The RIPERN course was new and set up between the Royal Flying Doctor Service and Queensland Health. The main objective was to legitimise what remote area nurses did.

Feeling far more confident, when an opportunity arose in 2002 to apply for the Director of Nursing (DON) position at Morven Outpatients Clinic, I eagerly applied and got the job.

Morven is a tiny town of 250 people with the nearest doctor 93 kilometres away. The clinic services a much larger geographic area including many grazing properties; halfway to Mitchell to the east, Charleville to the west, Augathella to the north and Bollon to the south. It sits on the junction of the Warrego and Landsborough highways in south-west Queensland so, for six months of the year, it caters to the tourist crowd as well. It was a dream come true. I threw myself into the role. There was a wonderful doctor in Augathella who became my mentor and friend. He visited Morven one day a week and we would still be seeing patients at 9 p.m.

Reflecting back is enlightening. I undertook my new role for all the right reasons and with wonderful preparation, thanks to the people I had worked with. Morven, although tiny, was and is challenging. I was required not only to see patients, but also to 'manage' the facility. I had no preparation for that side of it and I would labour long into the night trying to balance the books, do orders, check stock, rearrange the clinic a hundred times trying to get it exactly 'right'.

My work partner was officially the gardener/cleaner but

she became so much more, as I learnt is the way of the bush with work colleagues. I might have been the nurse, but the roles intertwine. I had no illusions of power in the position; we worked as team for the good of the community. If I got a little 'big-headed' I was quickly brought down to earth. One day, after an incident, I was relaying the details via the phone to debrief and seek support. Unfortunately, I said something like 'I'm here on my own', meaning that I had no doctor or other medical people to help me with the situation. When I got off the phone, she snapped at me: 'Who do you think I am? Just a piece of shit on the floor?'

It was very confronting and, at that moment, I realised I was never really alone in this isolated position. I had my work mate, visiting colleagues and the people of the town and properties for assistance. Since that day, I couldn't tell you how many times I have called on the locals to help me out.

In the beginning, life in health was uncomplicated. To receive medications for the clinic, I would write out a quick list and fax it though to Charleville. To pay a bill, such as electricity, I would just put it in an envelope and send it off. What happened after that wasn't my concern. All I had to focus on was the health care of the community. There was little paperwork, and corporate and clinical governance were unheard of out here in my little haven.

Morven was a bit like turning the clock back. People referred to me as Matron. I could never quite roll the 'r' as they did! At first I thought, *No way!* I hadn't even worn a sister's veil because I was university trained. I corrected everyone for about the first two years but then I gave up, realising it's about that old-fashioned respect of the nurse and the position.

RIGHT: The ever-resourceful nurse Roma Hollingsworth from East Gippsland in Victoria 'didn't regret a single day of living in the bush'.

LEFT: Pioneer nurses Mary 'Lil' Rogasch and Mary Madigan helped establish the first hospital in Halls Creek, Western Australia, in 1918.

RIGHT: Before there were cars, it was up to gallant bush nurses such as Alice Martin, from the high country of Victoria, to reach patients on horseback.

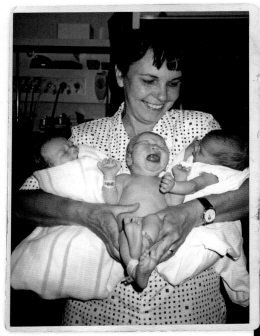

LEFT: Midwife Mavis Gaff-Smith once worked a shift in her maternity unit in the Riverina, New South Wales, during which ten babies were delivered in three-and-a-half hours.

RIGHT: Nurse and midwife Vanessa Page sees patients across a 200-kilometre radius among some forty Aboriginal communities in the Kimberley region of Western Australia.

ABOVE: The resilient Sister Fay Tilmouth, who raised her children while working as a nurse in the remote town of Andamooka in South Australia.

ABOVE: Christine Patt (nee Sinclair) recalls two years of 'hard work, spiritual growth, sadness, laughter and lasting friendships' as a nurse in Halls Creek, Western Australia.

ABOVE: Lisa Smith (front right) loves her job as a nurse in Pormpuraaw, North Queensland, where the kids call her 'Aunty', 'Nana', 'big mooki' and 'Miss Lisa'.

ABOVE: When Christine Patt (nee Sinclair) arrived in Halls Creek in 1965, nurses still communicated via radio.

ABOVE: Tere Garnons-Williams' work as a remote area nurse has taken her from the wilds of northern Canada to the mangroves of Arnhem Land in the Northern Territory.

ABOVE: Remote nurses aren't just inland: Stephen Fuller flies a helicopter to get to work on an oil platform north of Dampier in Western Australia.

Photo courtesy of Gerrad Meiers

RIGHT: Now retired, Mick Lanagan still assists at accidents on the Great Northern Highway in Western Australia when called upon. 'The Australian outback can be a tough place, but you have to be prepared for it,' he says.

Photo courtesy of Leon Mead: leonmeadphotography.com

ABOVE: Sue Stewart underwent a sea change when she quit her nursing job in Victoria to work in the remote Aboriginal community of Bidyadanga, Western Australia.

ABOVE: Sarah Emily Hamm and her colleagues had to trudge through a river with a wheelbarrow holding their work gear — including medical supplies and laptops — to reach Mapuru in Arnhem Land.

RIGHT: Clinical health practitioner Jo Appoo is passionate about her work in Central Australia and says she'll keep working for as long as she's able to.

LEFT: Catherine Ryan balances her dedication to nursing with her home life on a stock camp in north-west Queensland.

BELOW: When Julie Hogarth was physically attacked by a dangerous patient, her dog, Sabre, came to the rescue, tackling the man to the ground while Julie called for help.

ABOVE: Kathy Wooldridge samples some bush tucker as a relief nurse in central-northern Australia.

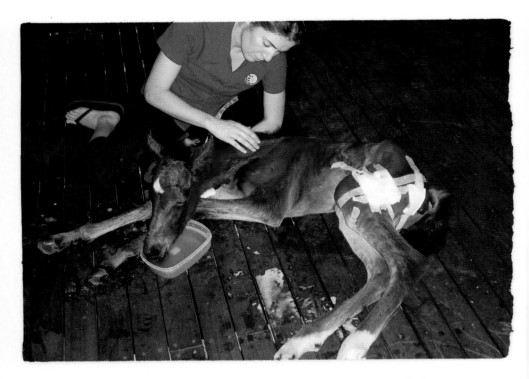

Shelley Munro knows that remote area nurses don't just treat humans. Hungry the horse was abandoned by her mother and set upon by dingos, then brought to Shelley's clinic. She didn't have high hopes for Hungry, but with careful medical attention the cheeky and loving foal was nursed back to full health.

Now when people call me the Matron when they speak to me, I appreciate it for what it is.

Many funny things have happened along the path. One day, in the ambulance, we ventured down the Bollon road to a truckie who was diabetic and was having a turn. We'd brought a number of men from town in case we had to lift the patient. He'd got himself out of his road train and was lying on the ground in the shade of the trailers, which were loaded with cattle that were bellowing very noisily when we arrived. I approached the patient and knelt down beside him to check him out. Just then, one of the beasts peed all over me! Well, didn't that set the crowd into raptures? They had tears in their eyes for days laughing at the Matron covered in cow pee. I did see the funny side eventually!

Today, health is changing. Instead of faxing off orders for medications, I enter my requests onto a database. My work partner, Sandra, does much of the administration as well as the cleaning and gardening but there is still a lot of extra electronic paper work for the DON to do. Every little thing goes onto a database. That aside, the basic nursing care I give to my community has not changed. I still look after them all, from babies to the elderly and everyone in between. There is a different doctor in Augathella in recent years and I am lucky because he has also become a valued work colleague and friend.

Sandra is my right-hand woman. Without her and this wonderful community, nursing in this medically remote location would be much more challenging. Sandra is also the honorary ambulance officer in town so, when I leave town at the end of my working week and return to my home in Charleville, Sandra takes over and attends to the health needs of the community. Where else would you get such great teamwork? I have a job where I am respected, appreciated and supported by my community. Working in Morven for the last ten years as 'Matron' has been a privilege and the best job in the world.

Jill Macdonald (nee Carroll), registered nurse, midwife, rural and isolated practice registered nurse (RIPRN)

Postscript: As a result of restructuring in Queensland Health, in November 2012, the DON's position was declared surplus and the Morven Clinic was downgraded and reclassified as an outstation of the Augathella Multi Purpose Clinic. The Morven community is fighting to have the decision reversed.

Swansong
QUILPIE, FAR SOUTH-WEST QUEENSLAND

Walking past the old glass cabinet in the hospital foyer, looking at the historical equipment in the form of glass syringes, bedpans, theatre instruments and old beautifully bound record books, my mind goes back to the days of veils, heat and dust. What a wedge of memories come flooding back, filled with much laughter and some tears. This is my swansong; my last day. Forty-five years of my nursing career coming to an end!

In 1967, having finished my training at the Alfred Hospital in Melbourne, my first posting as a graduate nurse was to Quilpie, a small, isolated town in far south-west Queensland.

It was my love of the bush that drew me back to this landscape and the embrace of friends met in my earlier childhood. Little did I imagine what incredible experiences were to unfold: some happy, some tragic and some just downright dramatic.

Within four weeks of my arrival I went on night duty. I was the only nurse in that rambling old hospital and at first I was scared, but after a while I enjoyed the quietness, and felt quite safe walking along the verandahs, past the many unlocked doors, to check on patients.

My first experience in dealing with trauma and isolation occurred when a woman was murdered. The matron and doctor at the time were socialising at the Club and didn't believe me when I described the emergency call I had received. So, when I notified them to say I had sent the ambulance out to do a halfway meet, they were furious. They soon changed their tune when I again rang to tell them that the ambulance had returned with the patient DOA (dead on arrival). Detectives and police arrived from Charleville within hours. It certainly was a very eventful night!

Before 000, we often received funny calls direct to the hospital requesting a trip to the post office or asking to be taken for chicken and chips at the café! One amusing night I received a call on night duty to a house in town. A woman said she had developed a terrible rash on her lower body. Thinking she may be having an allergic reaction, we quickly dispensed the ambulance to the house. I still laugh at the memory of the woman meeting us under the street light outside her house where she proceeded to drop her undies to reveal a pimple on her bottom!

At one time we had a severe gastro epidemic, particularly affecting young children and babies. There were so many babies admitted to the hospital we had to put them in card-board boxes and prop them up, doing a twenty-four hour vigil of nappy changing and feeding to rehydrate. Finally the exhausted staff succumbed to the virus, going down like flies.

Back then, there was no refrigerated morgue, so any deceased person had to be buried early in the day with many perfumed flowers and spray before it became too hot.

At times, there was a shortage of staff both nursing and domestic, so the patients would chip in and shell the peas or help fold the linen; a bit of occupational therapy! There were no silly regulations back then preventing such interaction.

I spent my twenty-first birthday on night duty! My parents had travelled up from Melbourne bringing cases of cham-pagne to celebrate an organised dinner at the Hotel Imperial. I wasn't allowed to swap shifts with a willing staff member, so we agreed that she would cover me by one hour so I could at least stay out until midnight. The matron found out about this arrangement and the following morning (which was my actual birthday) I was asked to attend her office at 9 a.m. I was duly hauled over the coals.

I had arranged to meet my parents and friends out at a friend's property for the rest of the day. On the way I had a flat tyre, which I dealt with, and then the car stopped right in the middle of the Bulloo River. It was all too much. I had a drink of tomato juice, crawled under a mulga tree and went to sleep, where the search party found me several hours later.

Years later, after leading another life, I returned to the Quilpie district at the tender age of fifty, marrying an old friend from those early years and settling down to live on 'Beechal', his property 150 kilometres from town. I commenced work at the hospital for a few days each fortnight, just to keep up my skills. Having practised midwifery for the past thirty-five years I was disappointed not to be delivering babies, but the newer doctors considered it unsafe with no backup if anything went wrong. However, for ten years I continued to perform antenatal classes, enabling contact before and after the birth. I loved doing this as it enabled one to engage and support young mothers who were often a long way from their families.

Over the next fourteen years, nursing played a pivotal role in my life; at first to renew contact with the community but later, when the drought of 2000–2010 occurred, it provided us a much needed extra income. It also kept me sane.

Travelling from 'Beechal' to Quilpie provided many challenges, particularly when it rained and the river was in flood. I had to take an alternative route on a wet-weather road. On one occasion I drove through a creek with no markers only to have water over the bonnet of the car and coming in the windows. I was determined to get through!

Due to massive rain, Quilpie was isolated for two weeks. There was a shortage of staff at the hospital, so I was flown to town in a helicopter to work full-time. What a sight it was to see the town surrounded by water. Once, on my journey in to work, I managed to get bogged. While finding rocks and branches to place underneath the wheels, I slipped over and fractured my ankle.

The following week I was to become the Acting Director of Nursing (DON) for six weeks. Because of the staff shortage I managed to perform the role from a wheelchair, in plaster!

Looking back, I recall the warmth of the community on both my arrivals in Quilpie. The first time was a great time to be young and free. There were many jackeroos and governesses on stations in the surrounding district in the late sixties, so it wasn't long before I made friends among young and old members alike, many who remain dear friends. With much partying, we attended polo carnivals, races, gymkhanas and polocrosse events. I recall Spiro Corones, who owned the newsagency, asking us what music we would like him to play on his record player. To his delight we suggested 'Zorba the Greek' so, thereafter, he would put it on loudspeaker and we would perform Zorba's dance in the main street, under the stars!

How lucky was I to meet and work with such fun-loving, beautiful girls who have stood me in good stead through good and fun times as well as the bad. In this small town the people are so privileged to have such a caring environment in which to be nursed back to good health or to be to be nurtured through aged care and palliative care for those dying. While it's sometimes difficult for staff in a small community because they know everyone very well, when an emergency occurs, all the staff in town turn up to assist with amazing teamwork and support, whether they're on duty or not.

As I look out across the gardens, I recall that, with no vet in town, humans weren't our only patients. We had one particularly beautiful female doctor who was to remain with us for nearly three years. Some local boys wanted to test her out and brought in a young unbroken colt that had a huge wound on its head. Much to the amusement of the inpatients, they threw the horse on the lawn in front of the hospital, tied its legs and sat on its rump. The doctor, who had no experience with horses, calmly knelt down and proceeded to suture the wound, with a staff member poised ready to grab her, if the horse struggled. The men were most impressed.

Today, as I complete my last shift, I can't help reflecting on the enormous changes that have taken place between the early years of my experience and now. Regulations in all areas have stifled lots of activities within hospitals everywhere. Imagine a vegetable garden in the hospital grounds, where some of the inpatients and members of the wider community could come and maintain it. They could enjoy the fruits of their labours in the form of nutritional food, to say nothing of the benefits of exercise and companionship.

However, the positives of new technology include better and more efficient diagnosis in the treatment of patients; the I-stat machine, which can assist in diagnosing a patient's condition within minutes with a simple blood test. Modern X-ray equipment and miraculous teleconferencing enables specialists to observe and advise both medical and nursing staff 'in the room' but from afar. These are just some of the modern wonders for people in the bush enabling better health outcomes.

I will walk out of this dear place – 'and bow and accept the end of a love or a season' ('Reluctance' by Robert Frost). This nursing life has stood me in good stead, providing friendship, laughter and tears, but above all the satisfaction of providing tender loving care to people from all walks of life, from the beginning until the end of life.

Dee Crotty, retired registered nurse and midwife

chapter three

NURSES AT WORK

Every day, nurses provide emergency and primary health care for people living and working in the inland of Australia. With their continued commitment, they help ensure the sustainability of the outback.

Out and About

HIGH COUNTRY, VICTORIA

I was called to see a patient who had almost succeeded in slipping under a fence, away from a cranky cow, but the cow had pinned her ear to the ground with the tip of its horn. I had nearly arrived there when a neighbour ran onto the road calling me to stop as his wife was choking.

I hurried in and fixed the wife up for a while with her head over an inhalation. After, I found the patient horned by the cow in bed suffering from shock. I examined the tiny hole in the ear, fixed that up, and hurried back to the other patient. Both patients recovered satisfactorily.

On my door there was hung a slate and pencil. I had to write where I had gone and the patients either came after me or wrote their trouble on the slate.

Looking out my back door one day, I saw across the field two men with guns trained on each other. As I watched, the man furthest away, over 100 yards (90 metres) from the nearer man, turned to say something to those around him and at that moment the nearer man shot him twice in the back then walked off into the bush.

I hurriedly threw the saddle on Jim (my horse) and rode round to the wounded man. When I was nearly there, a woman ran out waving a sheet, which frightened Jim. However, she rolled it up and I put it quickly on the front of my saddle. In a few minutes, I was examining the man on the ground. I saw where one bullet was close to the surface and cut that one out. Snow was now falling.

With two saplings used with the sheet, we made a rough stretcher and, tying the patient to this, it was placed across a car. With one man driving and another holding the improvised stretcher, away they sped through 25 miles (40 kilometres) to Dr Ley and his hospital. The patient was delirious and his legs were stiff. Doctor said the second bullet had lodged at the man's lung. He thanked me for cutting out the other bullet so speedily.

Extracts adapted from Memoirs of a Victorian Bush Nurse in the 1920s *by Alice Martin, registered nurse and midwife, transcribed by her daughter, Val Watson*

Never a Dull Moment
HALLS CREEK, KIMBERLEY REGION, WESTERN AUSTRALIA

Leaving my home on the farm at Temora, NSW on Boxing Day 1965, little did I realise what really lay ahead of me in the two years following, but to quote the old saying 'ignorance is bliss' I flew into Halls Creek via Darwin, leaving a hot, dry summer for an energy-sapping wet season in the Kimberley.

It was a neat township, with a population at the time of

approximately 100 whites and 500 Aboriginal people. I was pleasantly surprised by the cool, comfortable hospital with its wide verandahs and breezeway and by the inquisitive welcome of the locals.

Confronting the radio transceiver, however, was a different kettle of fish; it terrified me! It was not just the process of trying to decipher messages through the static, but knowing that half of the Kimberley population was tuned in to the 'Galah Session' to hear what was going on and what urgent medical cases were being discussed.

I vividly remember one particular case where an Aboriginal man presented at the hospital one evening in great distress with severe pain in his lower abdominal area. Gail and I sat with him throughout the night, poring over our medical books and coming to the conclusion he had a torsion of his testicle. As soon as we were able to contact the RFDS Base at Derby the next morning (no phone in those days), a plane was sent out to evacuate the patient.

The next morning with trepidation we called in to the doctor, only to be bawled out over the airwaves, 'Sister, how well did you examine the patient? He has the mumps!'

Most evacuations, however, were essential, including the wife of a station owner who was badly injured when she failed to negotiate a sharp bend, called the Devil's Elbow, on the road south-west of Halls Creek. The Shire President, Ernie Bridge, drove the ambulance, into which we hastily threw some medications, blankets and pillows; there were no stretchers in the ambulance. The retrieval was made without too many dramas; the lady was flown out to Derby and subsequently made a good recovery.

However, often due to a combination of injury, illness and distance, not all evacuees survived, and this left us with feelings of helplessness, frustration, grief and pain.

Our little hospital soon became the social centre of the town and hardly a night passed without someone dropping in. Right behind the hospital grounds was a mining camp, and many a night was spent playing cards, listening to records, making our own beer or chatting over a cup of coffee.

We never seemed to be short of company to go to the outdoor pictures. We'd leave a note on the front door as to our whereabouts, take our own chairs and hope that there wouldn't be a dog fight at a crucial time in the movie.

The running of the hospital went smoothly with Gail, Helen and I taking it in turns to do everything for a week at a time. One did the cooking for the patients and ourselves, one cleaned and washed, while the other one would attend to the medical needs of outpatients and inpatients.

We had a well-stocked treatment room, complete with X-ray machine, which we learnt to use quite adeptly. We gave the dental tools a good workout and the stomach pump, usually with Gail dry-retching in time with the patient. We had a great range of medications, bandaids and Mercurochrome, the latter two items in great demand with Aboriginal children who loved to ring the doorbell and show us a little scratch or sore, which miraculously got better after the application of Mercurochrome and band aids.

I fondly remember one elderly Aboriginal man who required injections in his buttocks. At the completion of the injection he would say, 'Tank u, tank u – my bottom tanks u.'

Race week was a time of great activity, excitement and

apprehension, the town busting at the seams with the influx of people from the stations from miles around. This increased the risks of brawls and accidents, however, depending on the number of patients in the hospital at the time, we were usually able to accommodate some visitors in the wards.

After the frenzied activities of race week (we also helped with the catering for the Race Ball) things would quieten down for a time, before gearing up for the Christmas party. Head office would send up boxes of gifts for distribution among the children from the town and surrounding stations. These were sorted and wrapped and then the cooking would begin: patty cakes of all sizes and colours and toffees, among other things. The problem was how to keep the toffee from melting or becoming too sticky, until we hit on the idea of using the morgue fridge! Fortunately it hadn't been in use for quite some time, so we set to and scrubbed, washed and scrubbed until it shone, inside and out. End of problem.

August 1966 was a special time as we had a visit from Rev. Fred McKay and Hamilton Aitken, the official photographer for the AIM. Three memorable events took place with their visit: an outside evening church service in the grounds of the hostel, a barbecue breakfast beside the creek at Old Town, followed by a short devotional service and the news that we were to have three weeks' leave to return to our families. What great news that was.

In between work and going on the Aboriginal reserve to teach basic hygiene and health care to the women and children, we found time for swimming in the waterhole, playing tennis and dancing.

There were quite a few keen tennis players in town and

many a hard-fought social match was won and lost. Mind you, broken strings necessitated the offending racquet to be sent to Perth for re-stringing.

One moonlit night, we realised we had an intruder in our food storeroom. Not really knowing if they had fled or not, Gail bravely stood outside the door with a didgeridoo in her hand calling, 'Come out whoever you are!', while we sent for the police. No-one appeared, but later when our stores were checked, it was found that quite a bit of food was missing.

The next night the police, the shire clerk and a couple of volunteers sat up on an all-night vigil in one of the wards, in the unlikely event that the intruder would return for further supplies. However, this did not eventuate. We never found the culprit.

On one occasion, we invited Slim Dusty, Joy McKean and Barry Thornton to share morning tea with us after one of their 'oh so popular concerts' where coloured shirts, high-heeled riding boots and big hats were the order of the day. We did enjoy the time spent with them. The next day saw us entertaining the WA governor for morning tea. Never a dull moment!

Being a keen gardener, I planted many trees around the hospital, some of which were still growing when I returned several years later. I also had a flourishing vegetable garden, growing tomatoes, onions, cabbage, cauliflower, shallots and pumpkins. We had to pollinate the pumpkins ourselves, as there were no bees to do the job. The biggest pests were stray dogs, who loved to dig in the damp, soft soil and often uprooted the vegetable plants.

As I look back at those two wonderful years of hard work, spiritual growth, sadness, laughter and lasting friendships,

I remember the words of the one who said, 'The initials of AIM should really stand for the "Australian Institute of Matrimony",' as so many of us met our future husbands while in these areas.

I thank God for bringing Rev. Fred McKay to Temora in 1965, showing slides and photos of the work of the Australian Inland Mission, as it was his visit that led me to Halls Creek – a journey that has had such a profound impact on my life.

Christine Patt (nee Sinclair), retired registered nurse

Australia's Frontline Matron

DARWIN, NORTHERN TERRITORY

Edith McQuade White commenced her nursing career at the Brisbane General Hospital, graduating in 1928. Having then done her Midwifery and Child Welfare Certificate, she became Matron of the Delta Private Hospital at Ayr in North Queensland. In 1937 she relocated to Darwin, where she worked as a sister at the Darwin Hospital before being posted to Katherine. In those days, this entailed a fourteen-hour train trip with an overnight stop at Pine Creek.

At Katherine, Edith was Sister in Charge, with several other duties in addition to her work in the hospital. For instance, she reported local weather conditions daily to the Darwin Weather Office. When required, at night she also set out and lit the paraffin flares on the runway for Dr Clyde Fenton, who used an aeroplane to visit patients in outlying areas.

She was later posted to Tennant Creek, a rough, frontier mining town where the hospital provided the only medical services between Katherine and Alice Springs, a distance of some 1180 kilometres. After seven months, she was advised she was to return to Darwin. Shortly thereafter, war broke out and she was informed that she had been appointed Staff Nurse in the Australian Army Nursing Service. She wrote, 'To my bitter disappointment the Government would not release me from the Northern Territory Medical Service [NTMS].'

Edith continued with the NTMS until the military authorities advised her that it had decided to establish a 1200-bed Army Hospital to be known as the 119th Australian General Hospital (AGH). Much to her surprise, she was appointed as Matron.

There were many difficulties for the hospital in the early period. The site selected at Bagot Compound was about 10 kilometres from the town, and as a temporary measure the army nurses were accommodated at the quarantine station travelling in and out every day in army trucks. By the end of 1941, new hospital buildings at Berrimah were sufficiently completed to move one medical officer, Matron White, six sisters and three general-duties men to this new site to prepare for occupation.

At the same time, the Administrator of the NT, Mr C L A Abbott, decreed that all civilians should be evacuated from Darwin. Following the fall of Singapore, the recently opened civilian hospital was seconded by the army for military use, which left the 119th functioning in three different locations.

This caused Edith great difficulty in administration and roster-
ing of staff.

The hospital received its first battle casualties on 18
February 1942, when eleven badly wounded patients were
admitted from a convoy that had been attacked the previous
day in the Timor Sea. The following day was one that Edith
would never forget. She later wrote:

The 19th February 1942 was a unique and memorable day
for Australia when she was attacked by enemy planes. At
10.45 a.m. an Air raid warning was heard just as enemy
bombers and fighters came over the town of Darwin. For
a few minutes it was not realised by staff and patients that
the armada of planes overhead was the enemy approach-
ing. The sound of the bomb explosions and ack-ack fire
soon disillusioned everyone. Patients were placed under
beds and those who could, made their way to the long
grass. Others scrambled to the few slit trenches which had
recently been dug.

Among the casualties admitted to the 119th AGH that day
were hundreds of cases of burns from the ships, the wharf and
the oil tanks at the harbour. The facilities for treating these
were poor and the nursing staff worked for thirty-six hours
straight until 190 of the most seriously injured were transferred to the *Mununda*, a hospital ship that had been hit at
anchorage in the harbour. Despite thirteen men being killed
and many wounded, the ship remained seaworthy and set sail
from Darwin at 11.30 p.m. on February.

Edith's impression of the scene was recorded as follows:

The wharf was still burning . . . as I waited with four sisters
who had volunteered to help the staff of the Manunda, *the*

whole scene was one of devastation. Bodies were washed up on the beaches. Men were collecting the dead and placing them on barges for burial at sea. It was so sad to see so many ships smouldering.

As a consequence of the attack, the decision was made to move the hospital again, this time to Adelaide River. Edith now had her staff scattered over an area stretching 130 kilometres from Darwin, in five separate locations. New logistical challenges arose at the Adelaide River site, with the result that yet again the hospital was moved across to the south side of the river.

Between October and December 1942, a number of groups of women and children from the islands to the north of Australia descended upon the 119th AGH. Edith wrote:

Their admission to the hospital presented many difficulties, so few being able to speak English. They were starving and very ill . . . there were a few deaths among the nuns who were some of the refugees. They had been hiding in the hills of Timor and were badly in need of clothing.

These people numbered well over three hundred and provided a particularly difficult nursing and social challenge to her staff.

Under Edith's direction, the nursing staff of the 119th demonstrated great skill and understanding in the manner they nursed their patients under extremely difficult conditions. During the remainder of 1942 and into '43, the hospital received many casualties resulting from Australian and American operations to the north, as well as from the bombing raids over Darwin and the surrounding area.

In March 1943, Edith White was promoted to Lieutenant-Colonel in the Australian Army Nursing Service, and was promoted also to Principal Matron of the Northern Territory. In January 1945, she was appointed Principal Matron attached to the headquarters of the Australian Infantry Forces covering the areas of New Guinea, New Britain and Bougainville. She was discharged from the army on her return to Australia in 1946.

Despite playing a significant part in the care and healing of thousands of men and women in the only part of Australia where major enemy action was encountered, she was never officially recognised for her contribution.

Adapted from Australia's Frontline Matron, *written by Rev. Arch Grant and included courtesy of Frontier Services*

All in a Day's Work
DARWIN, NORTHERN TERRITORY

I was a casualty nurse at Darwin Hospital back in the days when there was never enough staff and hardly a doctor to speak of. Back then, if you wanted a fast track to the top, or perhaps just a foot on a rung or two up from the bottom, Darwin was a good place to be. The order of seniority was simply who got there first and who stayed the longest, which is how, after about four months, I, a newly minted, general-trained nurse, found myself considerably higher up the scale than a newcomer who had three certificates and ten years' experience.

In the odd times when there was a lull, these highly skilled nurses might sit around rolling bandages or emptying rubbish bins while the 'old hands' like me did the nursing. Needless to say, many of them took a dim view of this and moved on.

I experienced things I might never have known had I followed a more orderly path through the ranks. We were run off our feet but what an exhilarating run it was. We used our wit and common sense, complained about double shifts and often ended up doing, or being, something entirely different by the end of the day.

One day, I was sitting beside an ambulance under a shady tree, 215 kilometres down the Stuart Highway, waiting to rendezvous with the Katherine ambulance. They had a patient who needed to have some tests in Darwin. He was old man with abdominal pain.

We got calls to lots of abdominal pains. The term covered everything from diarrhoea to childbirth. And who could argue? These things certainly caused abdominal pain. But it would have been easier if the request for an ambulance had added such descriptive words as 'because she's started labour' or 'because there's a bloody great spear hanging out of his tummy'. They'd have given clues to the sort of equipment we might need.

But this old man was the genuine thing. He certainly had abdominal pain but, as yet, no obvious diagnosis. The notes told me his tests were to see if his pain was associated with his treatment for Hansen's disease; that's leprosy. Terrific.

We did the transfer and headed back. It was not a good trip.

The driving was erratic. The driver was doing double shifts as he planned to leave the next month to join the hippie trail to London via Kathmandu and he needed the money. At least the radiator held water. On a previous trip into the bush I believe this same driver peed into the leaking radiator in the hope that he might get the ambulance to a vaguely remembered water-hole. Both he and the nurse survived so I guess he found it.

My legs were beginning to feel as if they were part of the ambulance furniture. I shook them and the stretcher moved. I started feeling sick from the heat and the fumes seeping into the back of the van. Before the outskirts of Darwin I was holding the patient in my arms and sharing the sick bowl.

The same day, and two hours after I was supposed to have finished my shift, I had to jump back in that ambulance and head back down the track to a spot where a man was reported to have slit his throat.

A few miles past the turn-off to Humpty Doo we found the man who would guide us to the scene. We followed some tyre tracks until they petered out, then we walked. It was getting towards the end of the Wet and the spear grass towered over us and made the whole thing just a teeny bit spooky. I was already a bit jumpy not knowing the circumstances that precipitated the cut throat, or even whether he was alive or dead.

Then, at last, a clearing. A body wrapped in a blanket lay on the ground beside a dead fire. A little further away what looked like a man was propped against the trunk of a tree. A brown paper shopping bag covered his head. I didn't have a good feeling about any of it and for the first time that day I was glad the driver had come with me.

I went to the blanket by the fire and lifted a flap. There was a grunt and an arm shot out and pointed towards the tree. I saw the blood down the front of this second man's shirt before I got to him, but his breathing was okay and he had a regular pulse. The paper bag came away easily and revealed an elderly man with a bushy grey beard. There had been a lot of blood but it was hard to tell what damage there was. I told him I would take him to the hospital. He mumbled an apology.

Back at the hospital, a woman in the waiting room saw him come in and told me his name. He's not well, she said, touching her head. I found his file in Records. It was a thick one. He has done this before. Poor, poor old man. Surely somewhere in the country, there is a psychiatrist who could spend some time in Darwin.

Not every day called for escort trips out and about, but every day was busy, interesting and challenging and altogether one of the best times of my life.

Margaret Hanlon Dunn, retired registered nurse

Stranded

BIRDSVILLE, FAR SOUTH-WEST QUEENSLAND

Having returned home, after about sixteen months in Oodnadatta, I found it difficult to settle back into the big smoke and yearned for the wide-open spaces and beautiful countryside as I battled the traffic in the concrete jungle. So when Wendy contacted me in 1978 to join her out in Birdsville

I jumped at the chance to breathe in a little more red dust.

We arrived in town and met the locals gathered at the airstrip waiting to pick up their provisions from the weekly plane. After a week of settling in and learning that we didn't have wheels, following the hospital car's demise in an accident, the other sister departed in her own jeep, leaving us high and dry. While plans were afoot to get another vehicle, we knew that nothing happened fast in the bush.

A few months later our 4WD arrived and I'm sure the first few tanks of petrol were laced with kangaroo juice. We enjoyed the freedom of being able to pick up our own groceries, the Flying Doctor crew from the airstrip and even have a picnic tea down at the waterhole without having to borrow the policeman's family car.

Once mobile, we reinstituted the clinic run up to Bedourie, some 190 kilometres from Birdsville as the crow flies. That township, nestled near the Hamilton Creek, which fed into the Diamantina River, was surrounded by mud flats and watercourses on two sides. Normally everyone used the straight, low road during fine weather but after heavy rain the low road became inundated and the higher flood road was the only way into Bedourie. Because of the unpredictability of driving on the clay road after rain, most people avoided going out of town if they could; that included us.

A couple of months later, I cancelled the routine clinic run because of bad weather and settled into a day at home with a good book. That was until an urgent medical call came through requesting assistance for an injured drover with a suspected broken leg. The drover was moving cattle to the east of one of the camps when he was kicked in the knee by a beast and couldn't walk. With the Bedourie airstrip flooded, the Flying Doctor had no alternative but to ask one of us to drive the 320 kilometres on the flood road to assess the man's injuries. So while the camp boss negotiated the 80 kilometres through thick mud and over fast-flowing creeks to reach Bedourie, I set out on my journey armed with a mud map from the local constabulary.

About three hours into the trip, I missed the turn-off and churned through crusty black soil until I became bogged when the surface crumbled under the weight of the truck. As the truck sank in the sticky quagmire, I removed my shoes and socks and rolled up my jeans before jumping out of the truck to survey the damage. When I saw that I was stuck in mud up to the doors, I made a cup of tea from our hot-water thermos before sloshing around in the knee-deep mud to plan my extrication.

Easier said than done, I decided, after the planks of wood and hessian bags disappeared into the muddy water, followed close behind by the prickly vines I'd stripped from a bush. A couple of hours later, I was exhausted from digging and playing in the muddy plains and despondently returned to the truck cabin a mud-splattered mess. I was grateful for the mud covering when the water-loving insects emerged at sunset and invaded the cabin in search of food.

Having raided the tucker box, I divided the meagre provisions into three portions as I didn't expect to be found until morning at the earliest. My thoughts went to the poor bloke with the broken leg but I was afraid that he'd just have to tough it out as I was stuck fast. As the quarter moon rose and the stars twinkled in the dark sky, I became more disheartened with the passing hours and rebuked myself for being inattentive and getting bogged.

A while later I thought that I was dreaming when I saw dancing headlights in the distance, but as they grew closer I knew that Wendy must have alerted the surrounding properties that I was missing. Sure enough, the two chaps had come to rescue me from my muddy dilemma and were relieved to see that I was still in one piece. With a concerted effort and engines revving, my truck was chain-pulled out of the quagmire and we headed to their homestead for a hot meal.

Being conscious of my responsibilities to my patient, I declined their generous offer to stay the night and continued my trip some 32 kilometres further on. It was after midnight when I got to the darkened town and the only light came from the back of the pub; I headed straight there like a moth to a flame.

After the hotelier recovered from the shock of seeing a pale-faced, mud-spattered apparition appear at her back door, she made me a cuppa. I could have done with something stronger but I was on duty! My patient had apparently treated himself to pain relief from the bar before retiring in his swag on the pub verandah. His loud snoring indicated that he was adequately medicated.

Early the following morning I checked him over before consulting the doctor on the radio session, and decided to leave him in town to rest his bruised knee for a few days.

While I was there, I decided to conduct a clinic before heading back home and my tardy appearance got a few funny looks from the townsfolk. Without a change of clothes, I'd crawled back into my stiff mud-caked jeans and jumper that morning.

In due course I arrived back at the Birdsville Hospital and peeled of my filthy clothes before hitting the shower. All in a day's work for bush nurses!

Sue Nilon, retired registered nurse

Down the Hole

COOBER PEDY, NORTHERN SOUTH AUSTRALIA

One never knew day or night what might come through the front door of the medical centre. Carol was in charge, and was certainly a very efficient and creative boss. It can't have been easy to coordinate such a changing and potentially critical scene, and I admired her for the way she did it.

One day, the phone rang and a panic-stricken voice communicated the latest crisis. A miner had fallen down an 80-foot drill hole and would need a shot of painkiller before being winched to the top. Carol looked across at me. Would I be prepared to go down a hole that deep via a narrow dirt opening in the ground not much wider than myself? 'Yes,' I said. 'I'll go.'

I collected the analgesia and a syringe, changed into my jeans, and went with the ambulance crew out to the Eight Mile mine. 'Don't let your feet hit the sides too much as you go or the dirt will fall below.' This instruction echoed in my head as I perched on the narrow piece of wood that was to lower me down the dim shaft. I clutched firmly at the ropes attached to my unstable seat, dangling my feet as straight as possible as the winch dropped me slowly downwards to the injured man waiting below.

He said nothing when I reached him. Pale under facial dirt and sweat, his body crumpled up under him, this man showed the pain and anguish that did not need words. I administered the analgesic, spoke encouragingly of the soon-to-come rescuers, and was raised upwards again the same way I had come.

Remaining to watch, I was so impressed with the efficiency and gentleness of the Coober Pedy rescue team. We flew our patient to Port Augusta that night for proper assessment and treatment, where he eventually recovered.

Audrey Aspeling, retired registered nurse and midwife

Hot Shots

HALLS CREEK, KIMBERLEY REGION, WESTERN AUSTRALIA

One of the tasks we had to learn was to take and develop X-rays. On my fourth day's orientation in Derby en route to Halls Creek, I had been given a lesson in taking them and printing them.

By March, we were having trouble with film clarity and

after a discussion by radio with Derby, we became more diligent in replacing the film bath regularly. It was a smelly job and, in retrospect, environmentally unsound; we just tipped it in the garden!

This, however, wasn't enough, so the Derby radiologist offered to come out on the monthly Flying Doctor clinic. I think he also wanted to see Halls Creek. We demonstrated what we did and he said our execution of the X-ray was fine and the machine was okay. We then developed the film. As the chemical bath was hotter than normal, we used to leave the film in for less than the standard time and in cool weather we adjusted for this. I developed a film and he was staggered at how quickly I was back out of the room.

'No wonder they don't come out,' he said. 'You have to leave them in each tank for five minutes.' The room we used was normally 38 to 44 degrees Celsius, so we suggested he show us.

He abandoned the development after five minutes and said he would sort something out. He then spent the day testing times for maximum exposure and minimum enclosure in the room. He went into town, bought a big red timer so we were accurate and advised us not to stay in there rinsing the film but to go out and use the garden hose.

Adapted from 'X-ray' by Michelle Meehan, registered nurse, AIM, Halls Creek 1970–1972, courtesy of the Kimberley Nurses History Group publication, Boughsheds: Boabs and Bandage: Stories of Nursing in the Kimberley

At Home in Marree

MARREE, CENTRAL SOUTH AUSTRALIA

I'd been doing relief work with the Child Health Service in Tasmania and then around country hospitals in South Australia, when I decided I was tired of living out of a suitcase and accepted a job with the Royal District Nursing Service of South Australia (RDNS) working at the Marree Hospital in the centre of the state. I came here for five years and thirty years later, I'm still here!

The RDNS was formed in 1912 and was one of the first nursing services in South Australia. In 2006, the Marree Hospital was taken over by the Royal Flying Doctor Service (RFDS) Central Operations and renamed the Marree RFDS Health Service. Technically we are still a registered public hospital with two beds, but only for short-term/acute admissions.

I am the only full-time staff member; however, I am fortunate to have two ladies in the district who are registered nurses interested in keeping their registrations current by assisting at the Service, which allows me to do patient transportations at times and to get away for study or training opportunities and holidays.

When I first drove up to Marree, the road was all dirt from Hawker and used to wind through Beltana. Now there is mostly bitumen all the way and it bypasses Beltana altogether. There are only 47 kilometres of dirt left to seal now between Lyndhurst and Marree.

There was a dust storm every day during the first week

I was here as the area was in its sixth or seventh year of drought. It was very dusty and, depending on the wind direction, I had to shovel dirt from the front and/or back verandah each day as the gauze screens didn't keep anything out.

Apart from the weather, I had to get used to using a two-way radio even though the telephone had come to Marree about two years before – this was just as the Ghan (train) stopped coming through Marree. There was still a passenger and goods train to the area until 1986 and Stateliner Bus used to bring the mail and passengers, but the bus stopped at about the end of 1988. From then the mail came up to Leigh Creek by air or road, and later by a mail contractor by road. There has been no public transport in or out of Marree since then, which can be a bit of a logistical nightmare for patients who don't have transport and need to attend appointments eight hours away in the city.

Even before the RFDS took over, they were doing regular clinic visits and emergency evacuations in Marree. I had to learn early on how to check the dirt/gravel airstrip before the plane could land, and where to put the flares for night landings and departures. These days Marree has a bitumen strip and electric lighting but we still use the flares if the generator fails. We get used to seeing the red belly of the RFDS plane around here – it lands in Marree on average once a week.

We've had lots of accidents over the years, though, fortunately, not many of them fatal. We had seven people in a motor vehicle accident once, which was a bit hectic, but most of them were actually okay, just shocked. One person was nearly scalped so the RFDS came and retrieved her. At one stage, I had so many people turning up with knee injuries, I was getting really good at predicting what their X-rays and tests would show!

It's always rewarding to see your successes walking around. One day, I was just going back into the room where there was a sick baby awaiting the RFDS retrieval team plane when she stopped breathing, literally just as I entered room. I was able to resuscitate her and get her away on the aircraft. She now has children of her own, which is wonderful to see. Many ladies have had babies over the years, but most relocate to a bigger town three weeks before their due date so they can be closer to major hospital services. So I've only actually helped deliver one baby since I've been here. In the first few years a lot of women went into premature labour and had to go south, sometimes for many weeks or months.

The first time I had to suture a horse, out in the middle of the paddock, I became very good at jumping out of the way. That was another skill I had to learn: treating animals. When you're the only person around who might know how, everyone asks!

There have been many incidents over the years, some of which I'd like to forget. I know one of the situations I had to get used to very quickly when I first moved to Marree was the amount of drinking and fighting. After a while, I could work out which nights I'd be working by the music that was playing around town. It doesn't happen so much now, but when certain music's playing, I still keep an ear out. I wasn't a great fan of Slim Dusty music when I came to Marree but I soon became one, when I realised I could relax when I heard it playing.

As you would expect, the population has changed over the years – well, some of the population. There are some that have gone away and moved back again. There are the past residents that come back for social events such as races, gymkhanas and camel cup, who are sometimes hard to recognise, but they remember you. There are lots coming back now with their own children, some of whom look just like their parents at the same age, especially at the local swimming pool. Yes, we have a school/community pool, which was installed the first year I came to Marree. I have been a supervisor at community sessions ever since.

We have quite a lot of sporting and fitness activities available. Night tennis is played over summer months since the local Progress Association had lights and fencing installed on the tennis courts. We also play indoor cricket under lights. We hold aquarobics in the pool over the warmer months and at present we're into Zumba in the cooler months. There are public swimming sessions seven days a week from October to April, and there is a town gym, a football oval (with no grass) and a fitness track next to it. When I first came, I was really into ballroom dancing so I used to hold sessions and even had some of the older residents coming along who usually didn't go out, but we haven't held these for many years. There is darts at the local hotel, which is really well attended, and not everyone who plays is an alcohol drinker.

There are actually a lot of people in Marree; we have a population of only about 100 (if everyone is home), but that number can treble when Lake Eyre is full as it has done twice in the past couple of years. Lots of tourists come to Marree to either drive in to or fly over the lake – it's quite spectacular.

I certainly didn't plan to be in Marree forever, but even though I don't have family as such in Marree, I feel I have a big extended family with all the friends I have made over the years. The school nominated me for a Children's Week award many years ago; I was one of the first community nurses nominated by a school and I did receive the award. I was a finalist in the Nurse of the Year in 1999 and featured on *Random Acts of Kindness* in 2009. I was privileged to be awarded an Order of Australia Medal (OAM) in the Queen's Birthday List 2009. Each and every one was a huge surprise but those things make you feel that you must be doing something right.

I am still enjoying the work and I hope not to leave Marree for a few more years. It is the people you meet as well as the lifestyle and work situation that make up the remote area experience. I can attest to the fact that this job is definitely not boring or monotonous, as you never know what is in store. There will always be lots of interesting characters to meet and challenges to face. It is amazing how your outlook broadens through an experience like this.

June Andrew, OAM, registered nurse, midwife

Outback Serendipity

BIRDSVILLE, FAR SOUTH-WEST QUEENSLAND

As a registered nurse, I was a girl on a mission to find excitement when I joined Frontier Services in 1982. Backpacking around Europe for nearly two years had not whetted my appetite for adventure so I decided to try the outback.

Given a choice, I chose Birdsville because I'd seen a model of the Birdsville Pub at the Munich Beerfest in Germany, and I thought it looked pretty cool. Within two weeks of my interview, I was on a plane to Birdsville, via an orientation week in Charleville. I didn't spend much time at the hospital though. I spent most of it with the local vet learning how to stitch up and treat animals. Just in case . . .

The nurses of the AIM and Frontier Services have, historically, been required to turn their hand to anything and my first job in Birdsville was to help unload the plane. I then delivered the next fortnight's fruit and vegetables to the hospital, where I introduced myself to the other RN, Leanne Hemer. Between us, we provided all the local medical services, supported by a monthly RFDS clinic. We also did all the vet work around the area. We were even expected to teach Sunday school, although I always managed to avoid that! We baked for social events and sold tickets in raffles. Happily, the Birdsville Pub lived up to all my expectations and I fell in love with one of the owners, Kym Fort, whom I eventually married.

Relocating to Adelaide, I undertook an advanced course in clinical nursing, followed by midwifery and then a neonatal intensive care course. In 1995, I returned to Frontier Services and the Birdsville Hospital for several years. I was much more dedicated to the job and enjoyed working with a young university-trained nurse, Kersten Davis. Kersten was committed to primary health care and evidence-based nursing practice whereas, by then, I was fascinated by the positive health care benefits of complimentary therapies such as aromatherapy. Our partnership worked really well because we were able to see the alternatives and provide the community with real options.

Of course, there were some challenges; you become so close to people in a small remote community that, while you personally share the joy you also share the tragedy. Our job was to provide whatever was needed to enhance the lives of everyone who lived in the Birdsville region. I always felt we made a very real difference; generally, it was an absolute privilege.

These days, I have retired from nursing, working instead as the general manager of the Outback Loop Birdsville and Innamincka hotels. With our hearts still firmly entrenched in Birdsville, Kym and I spend our time between Adelaide, Birdsville and Innamincka.

Jo Fort (nee Laurie), Retired registered nurse, midwife, neonatal nurse

Every Day's a Training Day...
CENTRAL AUSTRALIA

Growing up on the Tweed River in the 1950s, I never had any sense of racism at all. My nine brothers and sisters and I went to school with white kids and we were just one big crowd of friends. We'd have sleepovers at each other's houses and my mother would say she reckoned she didn't know whose head was what. There were dark heads and blonde together. We always knew who we were though. We're Bunjalung.

Someone once told my mother that the community should

be looking after her children. My mother is a very wise lady and she said, 'The only person looking after my ten children is me!' She didn't go for this kinship kind of thing. That's the way she was and that's the way I am. I moved my family up to Nerang when they were very little.

I'd been working in aged care on the Gold Coast, when I decided to go to Docker River to work in 1997. It's out past Ayers Rock, about 250 kilometres down a dirt road. I had no idea where I was going. I worked as a carer in aged care there. After about six months, an old guy asked me if I was Aboriginal. I said I was and then he said I should become a health worker. I had no idea what that was so I went over to the clinic and spoke to the nurse.

She explained it all to me and then we had to take it to the local council. They wanted me to train as well so I worked in aged care and two days a week I worked in the clinic on my own time. I did my course through Batchelor (Batchelor Institute of Indigenous Tertiary Education). Because I couldn't do blocks I actually said I'd do everything on the community and then, when I go on leave, I'd stay in Alice Springs and complete the Cert III (in Aboriginal Health Work). I was on a mission and did it in six months. (It usually takes two years.)

Then I applied for a job and ended up on Bathurst Island. I was a new chum! I had no idea where the Tiwi people were and, really, no idea what I was doing but I learnt fast. The experience was I went there for five years and set up and man-aged their first aged care program. And I started teaching Aboriginal girls to be carers in aged care. I'm very keen on training.

After that I went and worked remote for a while, then

ended up as clinic manager for Congress (Central Australia Aboriginal Congress) in about 2006. I tried to retire in 2010. I went home but the whole thing is I do feel for the people in the Northern Territory so I went back. I'm based in Alice Springs and I work wherever I'm needed.

As a clinical health practitioner, every day is a training day for me as sometimes I'm learning things and often I'm teaching them. A lot of nurses get sent up here who can't put a cannula in, who can't do an ECG, so I show them how. I encourage our young Aboriginal workers to do the training, to learn as much as they can, because they're the ones who'll be here long after the nurses have packed up and gone. The nurses don't stay too long because it gets too stressful for them.

I have managed clinics and still do sometimes when I'm needed. On a normal day I might do the equipment checks, set up and use the screening machines, do the ECGs and things. I can take blood, stitch a wound and put in a cannula. I do pregnancy check-ups and provide the health care people in the community need.

We attend accidents out on the highways or in the bush, providing patient care and treatment, assessing and making judgements about whether to medicate or ring the DMO on call. So I can pretty much do most of what a nurse can do.

One of the problems is, back in 1998, there were 400 Aboriginal health workers registered in the Northern Territory; today there are barely 200. It's got to do with lots of things. With the health workers, some of the people have retired or walked away because they've been made to feel like they're not doing their jobs for their people.

I don't get angry but I do get frustrated sometimes. I'm very passionate about what I do and I've been in the job for nearly sixteen years. The biggest problem is most of the nurses have no respect for and no understanding of Aboriginal people. They are there to do a job; they shouldn't get involved in family issues on the community. It's nothing to do with them. Some people are very narrow-minded. They wear rose-coloured glasses and they can't see the big picture.

I'm sixty-two now, but I look after myself and the passion will always be there so I reckon if I'm still okay I'll keep going. I don't work as hard as I used to. I go home for breaks now. Every now and then I jump on a Qantas plane and visit my girls back in Queensland or go see a friend in Darwin. I just turn up . . .

Jo Appoo, Aboriginal clinical health practitioner

Elcho Experience
ELCHO ISLAND, NORTHERN TERRITORY

I began my journey as a remote area nurse in the Northern Territory at the start of 2010. I was living in Melbourne at the time, working in community health, which I enjoyed, but contemplating a new direction. I came across an advertisement for a relief nurse in remote Northern Territory and immediately it spurred my interest. I applied to work with the Remote Area Health Corps and within a couple of months I

had a two-month posting to Elcho Island, a remote island, in
the Arafura Sea, right up in the top end of Australia.

Initially, I attended cultural training, in Darwin, at the
Charles Darwin University. However brief, it involved first-
hand knowledge of Aboriginal culture and being my first
exposure to the teachings, I was looking forward to building
on this experience.

The plane to Elcho was a small twin-engine aircraft that
seats thirty people; I had never been on a plane so small! There
was a stopover to Maningrida and when I stepped off the plane
I realised that I was in Arnhem Land. Although it was January,
in the midst of the wet season, the aridness of the land was
still apparent. The vastness of the land was striking and the
rich ochre colour of the dirt made the tall thin, trees and scant
buildings surrounding the airport stand out in contrast.

Finally, we arrived on Elcho Island, home of the Yolngu.
I was greeted by the health centre manager and taken straight
to my place of residence in downtown Galiwinku. As we
drove, I was confronted by a place with a shanty town edge,
houses scattered with hand paintings and open doors, families and babies and dogs spilling out onto their front gardens
and the partially bituminised roads. The locals walking on the
road were casually going about their daily business, while our
car weaved around them and the road-savvy camp dogs.

After my first day of trying to adjust to my new surround-
ings and work life, I took a trip to the local shop. On my
way I was greeted by curious onlookers, asking me, 'What's
your name, *yapa*?' Not knowing the word they were using,
I was happy to find out that they were calling me 'sister' a
common term to use for a female you don't know. With this

knowledge, I instantly felt welcomed.

Growing up in Adelaide and living in Melbourne, I'd had limited travel experience. On Elcho, I remembered being in the local shop for the first time and feeling quite overwhelmed. I was the only white person that I could see. They called me 'balanda' or 'white person'. To focus on one's skin colour was a concept that I had not really reflected upon before. Neither had I been seen and called on the basis of my colour. The confrontation of the moment was enlightening. It made me aware of the feelings that one would experience in another culture. Furthermore, it gave me a glimpse of what one might feel if they were the only Aboriginal person in a predominantly white environment, especially if they were referred to directly as a black fella, or Aboriginal. I had never thought about this before and the intensity of the moment was groundbreaking for me.

My house was a luxurious place. I was quite lucky to land this type of accommodation. Yet after a few days in the place, I noticed scratching coming from the airconditioner throughout the night and each night it was getting louder and louder. I took respite in the lounge room and later reported it at work. The local electrician was the one who dealt with the problem. Working on standard 'island time', two or three weeks later, he 'promptly' investigated the airconditioner and found not one, not two, but a whole family of rats in residence. He stated to me that afternoon that the problem was 'dealt with' and in my sleep-deprived state I couldn't wait to return to bed that night! Finally I rested my head. The next eight hours were accompanied by an orchestra of vocal rat sounds. They were trying to escape because they were plugged in with rat poison and so I listened to each one of their untimely deaths. Next day I slept!

The most impressive aesthetic of Galiwinku was the beach-front. The work office was set just behind 'beach camp'. The incline of the road heading towards the centre of town was lined with palm trees, which were often stooped to the right, due to a good storm. There sat, before the winding path to the shore, a solitary piece of playground equipment on which I often spent the late afternoon watching the sunset, talking to the local children or witnessing the foreboding clouds in the distance. The sunsets from that beachfront are still, to this day, the best I have ever seen and watching the local people drag their boats in to shore was really quite magical.

The camp dogs, however, were another story! I became aware of the beach-side dogs on my first beach walk. There was a pack leader to the beach camp crew; inherently asser-tive, he seemed to have human attributes, with the palest blue eyes that you have ever seen on a dog. On one of many long walks along the beach, they decided to turn on me. The weather was changing and a storm was brewing. The dogs col-lected together and started to run towards me, all ten of them! I had become aware of what to do in a situation like this: you stand your ground and even if you don't have a rock you hold your clenched fist in position above your head and scream 'Sha!', which literally means 'go away!'

But this situation was different and it was obvious that a simple proclamation of 'Sha!' was not going to work, so I ran for my life and screamed up to the beach camp for help! Momentarily I fell, slipping on a wet rock and cutting my wrist. Finally I heard a local lady coming towards me to help me. The surprising thing is that the dogs really listen to the local people; they have a strong level of control over the dogs. The lady who came to assist me threw rocks at the dogs and they scampered away. She was kind enough to join me on my subsequent walks along the beach, hurling rocks as we talked.

The outreach work was amazing. We would fly in a single-engine plane twice a week to small remote communities, to set up a clinic for acute and chronic health care. On Tuesdays we would visit surrounding communities by 4WD and on Thursdays we would commute to the other end of the island, Gawa. I had never learnt how to drive a manual car, let alone in 4WD conditions, but I learnt quickly! So I would set off in river-like conditions with a nurse who didn't like using the vehicle in 4WD, and an Aboriginal health Worker. The conditions were difficult, but I soon learnt which part of the road was passable. Surprisingly, I never got bogged. The best part of driving was listening to the health worker, who was later to become my *mari* (adopted grandmother), spot wildlife. Despite her glasses she had impeccable eyesight. For instance, she would exclaim '*bapi!*' in Yolngu Mathu and we would try to see where the snake was, watching her point in a particular direction.

Mapuru is a community that became dear to my heart. We flew to the small community on the mainland of Australia every Monday. During one flight to Mapuru the dirt strip was inundated from the recent 'yindi' rain or 'big' rain. However, the pilot proceeded to come in and when the back wheels hit the ground, the front wheels did not follow and so we continued to skid along the strip with the nose of the plane in the air until suddenly it fell forward. That was a bit of a hairy landing!

To get to the community, one had to trudge through a river.

We carried everything that we needed for the day at the clinic with us, all of the medical supplies, laptops, equipment and so forth, so it was quite the task to manoeuvre carrying the luggage while trying to avoid getting wet. Shoes were never an option! The health care team, including the visiting GP, had to roll up their pants and battle the river to get to the other side. There was seldom diesel to power the generator when we were operating the clinic. For privacy we used the clinic room and when taking blood it was best to line the person up in the direct sunlight, shining in through the window, to ensure best access to a vein. The level of humidity meant your clothes would be soaked with sweat within half an hour of being in the tin-encased room, so more often than not we'd move the clinic out on the porch or under the tree, which was far more accommodating for everyone.

During my visits to Mapuru, I observed one lady who would often rouse the people and get them to come along to be seen. She had a mop of ringlets that would gyrate as she waved her arms around, shouting in Yolngu Matha to the slow movers, to tell them to '*boundi!*' or 'hurry up!' She was a character who I instantly warmed to; she and the Old Man used to sit and talk to me, often asking if I was 'adopted'. Old Man would ask me every time I came to Mapuru, if I was 'adopted', and each time I would answer politely, 'No, I'm not adopted, I have a family.' Not really understanding why he kept asking, it got to the point where I was thinking, *Maybe he thought I had no family back home?*

After a few weeks on the island I had gathered that *balanda* often get 'adopted' by local Indigenous people to learn about culture and be a part of family, to form a connection and understanding of Aboriginal traditions. After having a chat with Old Man on friendship and family, I was happy to become 'adopted'. I was given a skin name and he bestowed me with the name 'Morning Star'. I was quite honoured and that is how the lady that I worked with, the senior Aboriginal health worker, became by kinship my grandmother or '*Mari*'. This was fantastic because we already were great friends and she was teaching me the local language, due to my interest and enthusiasm.

When I was leaving Elcho Island, I had a farewell with the health centre staff and friends I had made. As I was leaving, I was told that I had something waiting for me at the office, a present from my '*nandi*' (mother) from Mapuru. She had a large basket flown over on the plane, which she had woven for me with brilliant craftsmanship and vibrant Mapuru colours. I was delighted. I wanted to show her my appreciation. I went on a trip to Cambodia and while I was there, I visited a small village and found some beautiful handmade baskets. When I returned to Elcho Island the second time, I went to Mapuru and gave her the best basket that I had found. She studied the basket and was pleased, but seemed more excited to see me!

Experiences like these can be life altering and it certainly was for me. Since then, I have embarked on many more 'out bush' experiences and will continue working in remote locations in Indigenous health.

Sarah Emily Hamm, registered nurse

Dedication

KIMBERLEY REGION, WESTERN AUSTRALIA

I was providing a service in women's health to a remote area covering a 200-kilometre radius. This area consisted of about 40 Aboriginal communities, mostly quite small and inaccessible during the wet season. Many of the women in these communities had no access to women's health, unless they specifically made their way into town for this important check-up.

Most women don't have transport so when they come to town it is usually in a car full of other community members who all have their own agenda for being in town, and a woman wanting a Pap smear is probably not a priority for the rest of the car load. Because transport is always an issue, many of these women were either very overdue or had never had a Pap smear, which is why I took myself to them. With my Pap smear box under one arm and my head torch poised and ready, I made my way out to most of the communities over a twelve-month period.

I remember one day in November, which is a time of the year that is notoriously known as the 'build-up', I attended to a number a Pap smears in a small room with no airconditioning or fan. I can tell you, it wasn't only the clients' crotches that were sweaty that day!

At another community my only option was to provide women's health checks in a kitchen, once again without aiconditioning. Fortunately the fan was working; however, when the fan was going it blew the curtains out, which took away any privacy. So, just before attending to each Pap smear I would turn the fan off and hope that the sweat dripping from my neck didn't land where it wasn't supposed to!

I am very proud to say that I performed many Pap smears that year and to women who really needed them. It was certainly worth the brief moments of discomfort.

Vanessa Page, registered nurse and midwife

Looking After Bill
TARA, DARLING DOWNS, QUEENSLAND

I was working in the area of Tara on the Darling Downs as a home and community care coordinator. I was on my daily round of home visits and was on my way to see old Bill, who lived alone on his 1000-acre property. I had driven from a neighbouring property and entered via the back entrance down a track. It certainly wasn't what you'd call a road; more, deep gutters that looked like a parting in the bush.

After a cup of tea, a set of observations and a routine check of his vital call equipment (links through the phone line in case of emergency), I was on my way. It had been raining quite heavily a few days before but the water had receded from across the small bridge that was linked to the two dams on the property. The road was very muddy and slippery and there were cattle wandering across the paddock onto my path. I was creeping along in the car but all of a sudden I felt the vehicle slide and I had no control. The car did a total 360, going around a large tree to the side of the track, around a couple of bewildered cows and back onto the track with the car facing forward, gliding me out of the front gate.

I didn't know it at the time but old Bill was watching from his kitchen window. He was quite astonished at my car skills; little did he know they were non-existent at the time.

I stopped down the road to catch my breath. I looked out of the window to see a small wallaby peering at me from behind a bush. I thought to myself, I have just done this incredible driving feat and survived but all I have around to give me a standing ovation is a kangaroo. I gave it a smile and drove on to my next appointment.

Off to old Bill's place again, but I found he wasn't home. He had poor vision and shouldn't drive so I wondered where he was. I was travelling on a dirt road heading towards the next home visit when lo and behold old Bill saw me and pulled up in a cloud of dust in his worn-out ute. I needed to take his blood glucose level and check his blood pressure and with no-one likely to come along, we sat on the back of the ute in the middle of the bush and I conducted the health check. I asked him where he was going and he replied he was going into town to do a bit of shopping. Poor vision or not, he was determined not to give up the driving and no-one could convince him otherwise. I didn't argue because I knew I wouldn't win but it did get a mention to the local doctor.

It was always interesting to visit old Bill. On another day I decided to take my husband and baby to visit as he always asked about them and I knew he often got lonely. I pulled up in the car only to have a gunshot sound above my head. I looked up and noticed that the grandson was visiting and he had found old Bill's 22 rifle and was taking pot shots, from the verandah, of anything that moved. I sounded the horn to alert old Bill and I heard some yelling coming from inside. Bill hadn't noticed the boy sneak the rifle out of the house. The boy copped a whack over the head with the back of the hand. A few apologies were made and after that the visit went smoothly.

Tess Robinson, registered nurse

The Bus Trip

STUART HIGHWAY, NORTHERN TERRITORY

When on holidays, it's time to get away from it all and leave work behind. For a nurse, however, it isn't always possible.

I was in the Northern Territory, doing a bus trip from Darwin to Katherine and back. We saw lots of sights and even took a cruise on Katherine Gorge. We were all in tourist mode. On the way home, we stopped for afternoon tea. One of my fellow passengers sustained a nasty gash on his hand. If we had been within cooee of a hospital, I would have asked the driver to take him there to have the wound sutured. However, that was not to be, so I made do with the first-aid kit on the bus. The casualty was allergic to the antiseptic solution in the kit, so I needed to scrounge around elsewhere to find one he could tolerate, then steri-stripped the gash and secured the wound as firmly as I could. I then gave him strict orders to get it attended to at the hospital when we got back to Darwin.

At our next refreshment stop another passenger complained of stomach cramps and feeling faint. I'd noticed she hadn't drunk much water all day, and it was quite hot. She was pale and her skin turgor was poor. Managing a stubborn, dehydrated patient was challenging, but the driver and I kept her stable enough until we got to Darwin Hospital for proper treatment. So much for being on holidays!

I caught up with the bus driver again the next morning. A knowledgeable bloke, he was a walking encyclopaedia on practically everything Territorian. He told me I taught him something. On every future trip, he said he would find out who among the passengers was a nurse or a doctor.

Ruth Tye, registered nurse

Locked Up
PRISON SYSTEM, NEW SOUTH WALES

I'd been working in a low-security prison at Oberon when the opportunity came up for us to go up and relieve for a couple of weeks at Ampilatwatja, a community near Utopia, north-east of Alice Springs.

The prison at Oberon was 70 kilometres from town on a dirt road. It's an open prison, which means that it has no boundaries and the young offenders, all boys, who go there, are there on a trust basis. If they blow it, they go back into a lock-up. The young men there are on a kind of training program. They go for debriefing sessions out in the bush, learn to climb and abseil, go orienteering and generally learn skills that hopefully help them assimilate back into society and stay out of trouble. They are well supported and it's a pretty successful program.

I was the only nurse there, so I had lots of autonomy medically. The doctor would come once a week to see anyone I thought he needed to see. Anything at all suspicious, like an appendix for instance, we'd ship out to Oberon Hospital.

Before that I had a casual/part-time job at Mulawa, the women's prison at Silverwater. At the same time I was working a second casual/part-time job at a private boarding school in Sydney. I'd leave one job and go straight to the other some days so it was a real contrast.

Some of the boys were fascinated by my other job and asked lots of questions about the women. They were so totally different: the women at Mulawa were the toughest of the tough; they had committed the worst possible crimes imaginable.

The most interesting thing about the boarding school was the attitude of some of the mothers. The isolated mothers of boarders would pull out all the stops to get down there if their sons were sick or hurt. Some of the mothers of city boys would say, 'I'm busy. You deal with it!'

Isolation is not always geographic.

Rhonda Smith, registered nurse

The Nurse who Listened to Her Heart

BIDYADANGA, NORTH-WEST WESTERN AUSTRALIA

As you drive south from Broome to Bidyadanga, sweeping across the Roebuck Plains, the world unfolds before your eyes. Kite hawks whirl overhead, hump-backed Brahman cattle graze sacredly in the long grass. The sky is a shimmering blue, laden with humidity.

Two hours later you turn off the Great Northern Highway past a sign of multi-coloured handprints that advertises the local arts centre. This is a good sign . . . it points to hope.

The road into the community is flanked by red pindan dirt and dotted with fat termite mounds whose denizens forage at night for spinifex. Bidyadanga itself is neat, dusty and relaxed. People amble by. Nothing is hurried. Once known as the La Grange Mission, this is the largest Aboriginal community in Western Australia. Twelve hundred people live here. Among them is a relative newcomer who we have come to see.

Her name is Sue Stewart and she runs the local health clinic, a nurse-run clinic powered by Aboriginal health workers. Sue Stewart's journey to Bidyadanga began four years ago when she and her husband Barry were on a trip around Australia. After leaving Gippsland in Victoria, they headed west, hit Perth, turned right and made their way up the WA coast.

They camped one night at the Port Smith caravan park, a popular stop for grey nomads on the way to the pearls and pizzazz of modern-day Broome.

There that evening, under a starry night sky, they enjoyed a performance by the Family Shoveller Band, a well-known local Aboriginal group. The mother of one of the Shovellers got talking to Sue, invited her to check out the Bidyadanga clinic, and thereby planted a seed that grew into a new life. That woman was Christine Farrer, who works on reception at the clinic and who is now one of Sue Stewart's best friends.

Not long after returning to Victoria, Sue made up her mind; she wanted to give it a go at Bidgy. So she quit her job as charge nurse of the dialysis unit at Bairnsdale Hospital and told Barry it was her turn now. That was code for 'sell your trucking business and come with me'. Nicholson River Transport was duly put on the block and the Stewarts relocated several parallels above the Tropic of Capricorn.

As Sue drives me around Bidyadanga, pointing out the store, the swimming pool that helps to keep the kids healthy and the church, it's clear that this was a good decision. She is happy, she has simplified her life and she is using her skills to make a difference to people she loves. There is also a lot of laughter in the Bidyadanga clinic, which makes for a wonderful working environment.

Sue is patient, has gained acceptance and, while still occasionally perplexed by some of the cultural differences between black and white Australia, has learnt to go with the flow. 'This is how it is,' she explains, referring to a clinic where there are no appointment times.

She is proud of the strength of her new community, where traditional law is still taught. One of her grandsons had the time of his life when he came to visit Sue and spent a term at the local school. He was taken fishing, played footy in the pindan and discovered so much more than he would have sitting in a classroom back in Victoria.

Best of all, Sue's husband – old truckie that he is – has fitted in perfectly. Between fixing washing machines and catching salmon with the locals, Barry drives the patient transport vehicle on its regular runs between Bidgy and Broome. Unfortunately, those trips are all too frequent due to the reality of Indigenous health and its patterns of chronic diabetes, kidney disease and heart problems.

At the end of the day, we stop out the back of Bidgy at Jabilu Beach, where the mangroves meet a broad stretch of pure, softly windswept sand. Sue talks about fate and her experiences here as a remote area nurse. Yet there is nothing 'remote' about Sue Stewart . . . she is totally connected. 'That sense of community here is really important,' she says. 'Everybody knows everyone else and we all look out for each other.'

Tony Wells, Rural Health Workforce Australia

Postscript: Rural Workforce Agencies have traditionally recruited and supported doctors in rural and remote communities. In 2012 they expanded those services to nursing and allied health. For those who are prepared to make the move, there are some tremendous career opportunities for health professionals throughout country Australia. Rural nursing, for example, can be a stepping stone to the highly skilled world of remote area nursing.

chapter four
OUT ON THE EDGE

When the going gets tough, nurses get going, often well beyond the call. Intrepid, resilient, inventive, resourceful and downright gutsy, nurses pull out all the stops to rescue people and save their lives.

Nurse on Horseback

HIGH COUNTRY, VICTORIA

Alice Martin was born at Gisborne, New Zealand in 1891 when her parents, George Henry and Hannah Martin, were seconded to the Salvation Army. The family returned to Australia three months later, where Rev. Martin took up an appointment with the Methodist Church.

After leaving school, Alice undertook her training at Royal North Shore Hospital in Sydney, which qualified her for certified membership of the Australian Trained Nurses Association (NSW), of which she became a Life Member (Badge No. 4848) some years later.

As well as extensive experience in Sydney suburbs, including working in slum areas, she also spent time as a nurse and midwife in the Central Tablelands region of New South Wales.

She later replied to an advertisement for and was accepted as a Victorian bush nurse, in 1921. As a lone bush nurse, Alice had many extraordinary adventures and faced many challenges. While she occasionally got a lift with someone in a car as she travelled around her district, more often than not, she rode her horse.

The following text is in her own words . . .

One night, in 1922, I had been called to an urgent case in the valley. I felt very timid and wished that I had not to go. I had heard that the bush track down the side of the mountain was very steep and had slippery stones here and there and was dangerous even in the daytime. However, there was a patient in need so we hurried along following the guide to the patient.

After a couple of miles of riding, we came to the trail leading down into the valley. As my horse (a quarter draught) followed the other horse down the trail, he began to slip and slide then chomped his bit in a manner that told me he just didn't like it at all.

I breathed a prayer to God for help, and suddenly the horseman in front called to me over his shoulder. 'It's pretty bad going down here, but if you're nervy or your horse stumbles too much, just lean forward. I'll pull up my horse and lightly flick him with the spur. He will switch his tail and you can lean forward and catch hold of it. He won't mind a bit.' Surely an answer to a prayer.

I had the sense to take it as such and breathed, 'Thank you, Lord! Now please help me accomplish the impossible.' It was pitch dark, my horse was nervous, we could not go back, and I could not pull his head into the mountain as he might half-turn and then we would go over the deep drop backwards.

To lean forward and catch hold of the other horse's tail would be hard enough at any time, and it might annoy my horse. Just how could I do this and not fall off my horse into the depths below? As my horse stumbled, this and that rushed through my mind.

I held the reins tightly and slightly pulled on the left rein as I patted his neck and said, 'Good boy, good boy.' I slipped my left foot out of the stirrup and leant right forward, more and more along his neck and a little to the right, then I slipped my hand from his neck to his head, then with a 'Please, heavenly Father', I groped for the other horse's tail with my right hand.

The man in front had told his horse to stop and lightly touched his right side with the spur. At the critical moment, the horse flicked his tail and I caught hold of it, then without mishap regained my seat. My horse settled down, owing greatly no doubt to my own composure and so at last we reached the bottom of the trail safely. I have always felt glad that the leading horse's tail was so long. My horse didn't mind the other horse's tail brushing his face very much after all.

In the valley, the horses had to scramble over stones and wade through shallow water. This continued for a while then the man said: 'Do you see that light like a candle in the distance, straight ahead?' I said that I did. 'Well,' he said, 'that is where we are going.'

On arrival, I was able to save the life of a baby a couple of months old. The child would have died before he got as far as my place and the doctor lived 25 miles (40 kilometres) further at Warragal.

I returned home on my own next morning. The beauty of the valley was breathtaking. I felt like staying for a while and feasting my eyes on the beauty. What a different place it seemed to the one we had travelled the night before. No evil befell me; instead, I was surrounded by beauty. I felt I was ready for whatever awaited me at my cottage yonder.

Extracts adapted from Memoirs of a Victorian Bush Nurse in the 1920s *by Alice Martin, registered nurse and midwife, transcribed by her daughter, Val Watson*

Riding the Seesaw

WESTERN AUSTRALIA

One day we were in one of the communities and we had a
Canadian nurse working with us. We had to bring in a very
tall man after an accident. We didn't have an ambulance, of
course, just an old troopy. Anyway, we put the patient in the
back. We couldn't fit him in so we left the door open with his
feet hanging out the back.

He was very sick and we were concentrating on getting him
back so we could stabilise him. Vikki was driving the troopy, I
was perched up near his head because we had to maintain his
airway, and the Canadian was down the back helping to keep
the patient secure. We went round a corner and the Canadian
just gently rolled out the door and onto the road. We stopped,
he dusted himself off and climbed on board again and we got
the patient back to the clinic. We got him stabilised and flew
him out to Perth.

After he'd gone, we debriefed; talking about it amongst
ourselves, we replayed the roll out the door several times. By
then, we were all falling about with almost hysterical laughter.
It was such a relief and it's part of the process of coping.

The patient died a few weeks later.

Sometimes it's like a seesaw.

Rhonda Smith and Vikki Robertson, registered nurses

On the Edge

HIGH COUNTRY, VICTORIA

One of my bush-nursing centres was Dargo, Victoria, 85 miles (137 kilometres) from the nearest town and doctor. One day, I was taking a very ill patient to the doctor by car. There were many dangerous hair-pin bends on the road.

At one place for 4 miles (6.5 kilometres), the road was very dangerous, winding down steeply with many hair-pin bends. On one side there was a cliff face and on the right-hand side, a steep precipice. The road slanted slightly towards the cliff and along here there was a trickle of water. It was impossible for vehicles to pass.

On this 4-mile stretch, every driver wishing to go up or down had to telephone ahead to find out if the road would be clear. They would ring either from the house at the bottom to the house at the top, if going up, or vice versa if going down.

My driver had telephoned from the top house the day we were going down. When we were about halfway down, great was our dismay to glimpse, on one of the bends, a wagon with four horses coming up. The driver had failed to ring up. Neither of us could go backwards and we could not turn round; the road was too narrow and it was impossible.

My car driver applied the brakes. While the car slipped past the first two horses, the second three horses remained in front of the car. The engine stopped right under the horse on the left with its front legs lifted (one on each side), and its head came within a foot of the front glass. Its distended nostrils and frightened eyes seemed to come within a few inches of my face!

The car driver backed from under the horse, then we had to lay the patient in the trickle of water on the side of the road against the cliff face so he could not roll over the precipice (about a 200-feet [60-metre] drop). The driver of the wagon unhitched the four horses and I breathed a prayer as I led them past the car and as near to the cliff face as possible.

I spoke soothingly to them all the way. They were frightened but remained quiet while the two men took two wheels off the wagon and then miraculously managed to turn the wagon onto its side towards the cliff. The car driver then took his life in his hands as he performed another miracle, driving the car past it. I saw the car take the bend on three wheels. I saw the right-hand side back wheel, for a few seconds, actually out over the precipice. We reloaded the patient, helped the man put the wheels back on and continued on our way.

Extract adapted from Memoirs of a Victorian Bush Nurse in the 1920s *by Alice Martin, registered nurse and midwife, transcribed by her daughter, Val Watson*

Bushfire

HIGH COUNTRY, VICTORIA

Bushfires are just awful at any time, anywhere, and it is advisable to keep as far as possible from their path, but it came about that one day my faithful horse and I just had to take the great risk of facing a bushfire. What a mighty monster it looked, as it rushed ahead, as if determined to burn up everything in its path.

I had to visit a farm to take the urgently needed medicine. The heat and smoke were with us as we left home. The further we travelled from home, the nearer we came to the bushfire. Then, as we actually turned onto the road leading to the patient's property and home, the heat was terrific and the roar was frightening.

The fire was on both sides of the road and as the wind veered, the flames in the high trees rushed towards the road and each other. Neither my faithful horse nor I liked it at all but we kept on and at last turned on to the clearing where the grass was free from the big trees, but the smoke and heat kept with us down the hill.

My horse, Teddy, would slip and slide and when we reached the bottom of the hill, we went through the creek then clambered up the steep bank and so to the house. I gave the medicine to the patient and said: 'I can't stay at all, dear. You'll find all the necessary directions in with the medicine. I hope rain will come very soon. Do stay inside with the children because there are plenty of flying, burning, bark twigs and leaves.'

We came down the hill again to the creek and felt the terrible heat. Teddy clambered safely up the steep bank and so on to the road, which had the roaring fire on both sides, very near the road. We actually had to go through the flames in places where the fires had crossed the road.

It was only a dirt road so Teddy's feet were safe but, of course, the road must have felt shocking. I had to lie on my horse's neck and even when I tried to encourage him, my throat felt burning hot. Naturally we were both frightened and knew there was terrible danger.

At last we turned on to our home stretch. We did not catch on fire and my horse did not fall or give in. I did not fall off his back or lose my nerve either. The heat was bad enough along the home stretch but there was a field of wheat now between the fire and us.

We thankfully arrived home. As I undid the gate Teddy whinnied quietly. I felt an answering sob in my throat. We were both sopping wet of course, owing to the intense heat, but so glad to be home again after our mighty adventure. And we were still the very best of friends; tried and true was my faithful Teddy.

Extracts adapted from Memoirs of a Victorian Bush Nurse in the 1920s *by Alice Martin, registered nurse and midwife, transcribed by her daughter, Val Watson*

Outback Rescue

OODNADATTA, NORTHERN SOUTH AUSTRALIA

After my acceptance into service with the Australian Inland Mission, now called Frontier Services, I joined the enthusiastic team of caring people who strove to make a difference in the lives of folk living in remote Australia. After ten years in the public health sector I was up for a challenge and there was no better way than to roll up my sleeves and jump right in. Following my commitment ceremony in April 1976, I was on my way to Oodnadatta, an isolated town in northern South Australia, to take up a posting at the hospital. The rail link was the only means of transport for groceries and other heavier items that couldn't be transported on the small weekly mail plane.

Even after attending an orientation program in Adelaide before heading up north, the idea of running an outpost hospital without a doctor on site was a unique nursing experience and one that I found both terrifying and invigorating at the same time. Thanks to my predecessor, who guided my faltering footsteps during those first couple of months, I was able to overcome many of the hurdles of adjusting to life in an isolated town in the middle of nowhere.

Being in a small place, we relied on many people including the wonderful people in Adelaide and head office, who helped sort out problems when they arose. The townsfolk contributed in many ways to the running of our clinic by doing repairs to the car, building, radio and so forth, while we contributed to their health and wellbeing. The community services officer helped our indigenous community with financial assistance and employment opportunities, while the police kept order in the town. The storeowner supplied provisions and the postmistress kept us in touch with the outside world. The teachers and hostel workers cared for the children and liaised with us when concerned about their health. We all played our part in making this small town home.

There was no way that I could have envisaged the work involved when I took on the role as jack-of-all-trades within the hospital environs, for not only were we the administrators of the facility, but also the doctor, nurse, social worker, mothers and babies support person, dentist and local vet. This is not to mention conducting the Sunday school religious program for the kids and counselling folk in need.

As our medical support came from the Royal Flying Doctor Service based four hours' flying time away, we each depended on our partner to help institute first-line treatment when a seriously ill patient presented. Though we could contact the medical personnel at the RFDS base within ninety seconds, we often relied on a coordinated effort to stabilise the patient for transfer. We were on call twenty-four hours a day, seven days a week, but still had plenty of time to join in the social activities and contribute to the town's running through the local government body.

When on duty, the sister conducted the radio sessions on the cumbersome double-sideband radio transceiver and made contact with the surrounding properties for any outstanding medicals before opening the airway for general chit-chat, which might include taking shopping orders for the store, or chasing up stock truck arrival and cattle train departure times. Coming from the city, I initially found working the radio network a little daunting, especially when the local vernacular hissed across the static-laden airways. I often felt inadequate when I had to ask for the message to be repeated. We were often the only link for the isolated homestead owners to avail themselves of medical advice and treatment without having to travel hundreds of miles, and this was one of our more important roles in servicing the remote outback.

With this in mind, I am reminded of a call I received on the

early-morning session about a sick little boy on a property 100
kilometres away. Having previously managed his older sister's
respiratory infection by radio medical calls and using the antibiotics from the property's Flying Doctor medical chest a few
days earlier, I assumed the young boy's illness came from her,
so recommended the same treatment.

When I tuned in on the radio a few hours later, Pat sounded
quite anxious about her three-year-old son's breathing problem, which was getting worse as time passed. The thing that
alarmed me more was that Joshua had asked his mum if he
was going to die. I knew that he must be in real trouble to ask
that question, so advised Pat to get hold of the Flying Doctor
immediately. I listened to the medical call and offered to review
Josh as I was closer and the doctor agreed that time was of the
essence to treat this little kid. With my initial plan to meet the
family halfway to give the toddler medication abandoned after
hearing the news that Pat's husband had taken the last vehicle
to muster cattle, I moved on to plan B of hightailing it out to
the homestead.

While my colleague, Wendy, jogged around to the community nurse's place to rope her in to accompanying me on the
trip, I filled the vehicle from our 44-gallon fuel drum using a
hand-pump then packed the spare wheel, fuel jerry-can, medical chest and oxygen cylinder in the back ready for a quick
departure. We took off while Wendy contacted the RFDS base
to advise them of our ETA at the property, adding that I'd
contact them as soon as I'd seen Joshua. This meant interrupt-
ing the School of the Air transmission to update the medico.
Wendy took over the running of the hospital and monitored
the radio in case Pat called again before we arrived.

Fearing the worst and without a portable radio in the station wagon to update us in transit, I put the pedal to the metal to get there as quickly as humanly possible. Being familiar with the lay of the land and its dirt, gibber stone-strewn road, we arrived at the homestead in just over an hour and pulled up in a cloud of dust. Pat had seen our red-rooster tail of dust a few kilometres out so was waiting for us on the open verandah and quickly ushered us inside to see her son. Little Joshua's laboured breathing could be heard from the hallway and I knew that things were serious even before I saw his heaving chest and blue lips. I quickly checked if he had an obstructed airway, then gave him a dose of broncho-dilating Ventolin and face mask oxygen before making contact with the Doc for advice and a management plan.

Having heard my clinical finding, the doctor thought that Josh probably had bronchiolitis, a condition that produced thick mucus that could obstruct a small child's airway. He recommended that we take him back to the hospital for treatment in a high-humidity oxygen tent. We departed with the whole family in tow and returned to town at a more sedate pace. As Wendy had been monitoring the medical call and knew we needed the mist tent, she'd assembled the equipment in readiness for our arrival.

Wendy and I took it in turns in working the night shift and, after three days of high humidity and antibiotics, little Josh's condition had improved enough to come out of the mist tent and sleep beside his mum. By day five Josh was on the mend and we discharged them home when Dad returned from mustering. Armed with instructions for first-line care if Josh became unwell again, his grateful mum gave us both a hug before heading home. We continued monitoring Joshua's condition for several more days on the radio network and he recovered fully.

Sue Nilon, retired registered nurse

Beyond the Call

HALLS CREEK, KIMBERLEY REGION, WESTERN AUSTRALIA

In 1912, the Rev. John Flynn gained the approval of the Presbyterian Church to set up the Australian Inland Mission (AIM). John Flynn was appointed its superintendent, a position he retained until his death in 1951.

I grew up in a family of parents and grandparents who supported the Rev. John Flynn's endeavours to get a Flying Doctor Service started, along the lines suggested by my uncle, Lieutenant John Clifford Peel, whose letter to John Flynn, in 1917, convinced him that aeroplanes could be used to assist medical aid in outback Australia. That dream was later realised, in 1928, when the Aerial Medical Service performed its first mercy flight. Initially part of the AIM, it later became the Royal Flying Doctor Service (RFDS), an independent and world-renowned organisation.

The AIM Hospital at Halls Creek, in the Kimberley region of Western Australia, was established in 1918 in response to an event which became famous. A year earlier, James Darcy, a stockman at Ruby Plains Station, 75 kilometres south of Halls Creek, was mustering cattle when he fell from his horse and was seriously injured. When his friends found him they took him to Halls Creek (the journey took twelve hours) but there was neither a doctor nor a hospital in the town. The local postmaster, Mr Tuckett, realised Darcy needed immediate medical attention. Using only morse code, a surgeon in Perth, Dr Holland, diagnosed Darcy as having a ruptured bladder. He had to be operated on immediately. Messages flashed back and forth in morse code.

'You must operate.'

'But I have no instruments.'

'You have a penknife and razor.'

'What about drugs?'

'Use permanganate of potash.'

'But I can't do it.'

'You must.'

'I might kill the man.'

'If you don't hurry, the patient will die first.'

Tuckett strapped Darcy to the table and began operating according to instructions he received by telegraph. The operation took seven hours – with no anaesthetic. A day later complications set in. It became obvious that a doctor would have to come to Halls Creek. Dr Holland took a cattle boat from Perth to Derby and then travelled the last 555 kilometres by T-model Ford, horse and sulky and foot. He finally arrived in Halls Creek only to find that Darcy had died the day before, though not from his surgery.

The Rev. Dr John Flynn realised that Halls Creek was another remote place needing a hospital.

With nursing for the Australian Inland Mission (AIM) always in mind, I commenced my general nursing training at Geelong Hospital and completed midwifery training at the Queen Victoria Hospital in Melbourne in 1945. During that time I met my husband-to-be, who was an Air Force officer. I had already applied and been accepted for service with the AIM and was awaiting an opportunity to go to Halls Creek.

At this time AIM nurses were appointed for two years. We were expected to fulfil this term without holidays and had to be very fit! It was also desirable to be very good friends. During my training in Geelong, I met Marjorie McKean, who was also training with a view to working for the AIM. We were both members of the Presbyterian Church and followed the work of Flynn of the Inland very closely. In April 1946 Marjorie and I were appointed to Halls Creek.

After almost a fortnight of travelling by train and plane, we finally arrived at the Halls Creek aerodrome about 2.30 in the afternoon. We were met by the Secretary of the Roads Board, who was also Secretary of the Hospital – a Mr Arty O'Leary. Transport from the aerodrome to the town, a distance of 16 kilometres, was by the Roads Board's tip truck, driven by Arty who was very deaf and only had one eye. We sat in the front seat and the two retiring nurses sat in cane chairs on the back. The road was incredibly rough but the time went quickly as Arty questioned us on our ability to make bread, milk goats and pull teeth!

Our day commenced at 6.15 a.m. when we answered the roll call on our pedal radio to Wyndham, 400 kilometres away. The call sign of the base there was 8WY. This session was the only one where we could get clear reception, so if we needed advice from a doctor we had to use that session. To pedal the radio for transmission was like riding a bicycle uphill, so if we had a lengthy report to give, one of us would pedal while the other spoke.

At this time there was no actual Flying Doctor Service in the Kimberley region. A doctor from Broome or Derby called at Halls Creek every six to eight weeks. By road, Broome was the best part of 800 kilometres away, Derby a bit less. He came on the regular weekly flight of the MacRobertson-Miller Airline (MMA). The plane arrived at Halls Creek about 5 p.m., stayed overnight and left at 5 a.m. next day. We usually had a number of patients waiting to see the doctor and these had to be examined by the light of a hurricane lantern. If possible, we 'saved up' any dental extractions for the doctor, but when this was not possible we pulled the teeth ourselves.

If a doctor was unable to come to Halls Creek and a patient needed his attention, we took the patient to either Derby or Wyndham on the MMA plane. Once, however, Marjorie and I had to do an operation ourselves via radio instruction. It was an elderly man who had bladder trouble and just as Dr Holland told Mr Tuckett all those years before, our doctor in Wyndham said, 'Well you'll have to operate, sister, or he will die.'

And I thought to myself, *Well, he still might die.* But he said, 'Wheel his bed so that you can hear the radio and I will give you instructions.'

The two policemen came over to hold the patient down. The doctor gave us instructions and we made the incision, got the catheter into the bladder and, wonderful news, the water started flowing and there was great relief all round. We did feel very proud. It was quite a nerve-racking thing to do.

Usually though, we had time to get a patient to Wyndham or Derby, which meant that one nurse had to travel with the patient and would be away for a week, while the other kept things going at Halls Creek. In one extreme emergency we had to get an RAAF plane to come from Darwin.

The AIM office teams in the capital cities of Australia kept us supplied with books and magazines for anyone who needed reading matter. These were very popular, especially with the 'Old Timers' who lived on the outskirts of the town and came regularly to collect them and have a chat with us.

When we were not busy at the hospital, life was very relaxed in Old Halls Creek. We played tennis each afternoon and this was a great time for the townspeople and the staff who came in from the aerodrome. We enjoyed the beautiful sunrises and sunsets. I shall never forget some of the thunderstorms we experienced. It was wonderful to see Hospital Creek and Halls Creek running so high after being dry for months. After the water subsided we would go down the Hospital Creek with our Aboriginal help, Daisy, and look for gold specks. We were not very successful, but Daisy's sharp eye would always produce something worthwhile.

Each year at Christmas, before the wet season set in, we held a party for the children on outlying stations as well as those in town. Santa Claus would arrive, very hot in red suit, whiskers and all.

The annual race meeting was the main event of the year. This was held to raise funds for the AIM and Flying Doctor Service. For four days the town's activities centred around the racecourse, which was 16 kilometres from Old Halls Creek, near the site of the new town. It was hoped that we would not have any patients in the hospital at that time. However, at one time we did have an elderly man with a heart complaint and he insisted that we should all go. So a comfortable bed was made up on the back of the Roads Board's tip truck for him so we could take him with us and a great time was had by all.

We spent two and a half years in Halls Creek. In October 1948 Sister McKean and I left Halls Creek for home and soon after I was married.

I feel very privileged to have lived and worked for the AIM in Old Halls Creek.

Dulcie Andrew (nee Peel), retired registered nurse

Emergency Call

KALTUKATJARA, (DOCKER RIVER),
NORTHERN TERRITORY

It was 4.30 p.m. on Friday afternoon and we were thinking of going home when the call came. Relayed via several people, none of whom spoke English as their first language, it seemed that there had been an accident on the dirt road, about 150 kilometres away.

We were two remote area nurses (RAN) based in the community providing all the general day-to-day health care for a remote Aboriginal population of approximately 300 people.

The nearest medical help and hospital was an eight-hour drive away, mostly on dirt roads. A possible accident with no other details meant we had to leave the community to investigate.

An RAN has to think of much more than the immediate emergency response. The ambulance was a 4WD Toyota troop carrier, fitted out with one stretcher and two small oxygen bottles. There are no other emergency services or retrieval support services in the area and the ambulance usually doubled as a passenger vehicle. If the accident was 150 kilometres away, then it had already happened more than an hour before we received the news. The dirt roads and sand hills meant time-wise it would take at least two hours to get to the possible site. All the emergency equipment for responding to off-site situations was kept stored in their packs in the cupboards and needed to be loaded into the ambulance. Loading them in the ambulance reduced available seating from six to four, with one patient lying down.

We did not know how many patients were on site or how critically injured they were. A plan had to be made to deal with the broken-down vehicles that may have been obstructing the road.

I loaded the ambulance, collected food and water to sustain us through what was going to be at least another four hours added onto our just-completed eight-hour day, and advised the Royal Flying Doctor Service (RFDS) of the situation. The closest police were three hours' drive west, while the potential accident was two hours' drive east; it would take police five hours to get to the site, if they were available to come and not tied up with other duties. Wendy went off to locate a community member with a utility who was happy to travel with the ambulance – the utility could carry things required from the crash site, which wouldn't fit in the ambulance.

At 5 p.m. we drove out of the community, heading east. There was no mobile phone coverage and the satellite phone reception was patchy to say the least. We drove on as the sun began to sink, to find our patients just on dusk (about 7 p.m.) scattered over the road. A group of tourists were travelling around Australia on motorbikes and had come to grief on the sand hills of the road. Three were intact, another had injured his ankle and one was lying on the road, conscious, with breathing difficulties. We swung into action most efficiently, uncovering his chest for an assessment, doing observations, commencing intravenous fluids, giving intravenous morphine for pain relief, and tucking him up in thermal blankets to preserve body warmth. The sun had set and it was becoming colder and colder, especially on the sand. We had him all nicely stable and looked around for help to put him on the stretcher and take him to the clinic.

To our horror we suddenly heard and saw all his friends on their motorbikes and our assistant in his ute driving east, leaving us alone on the road with the patient. Did they think we were okay and they could leave? Regardless, we needed their help, so Wendy set off in hot pursuit in the ambulance, while I stood on the dirt road, holding a drip in the air and reassuring the patient that everything would be okay. The abandoned stretcher stood forlornly by, awaiting its load.

Thirty minutes later the ambulance returned with the ute. In his innocence, the assistant had gone to show the tourists a good camping spot for the night; it was too dark and dangerous to travel any more on the road. They intended to return to the bitumen the next day and continue their journey across Australia by another route. We loaded our patient on the stretcher and returned to the clinic for him to be evacuated by RFDS. He turned out to have a pneumothorax and after a short stay in hospital went back to his own home town. His motorbike came back to the community with us in the back of the ute and travelled home on the store truck a month or so later. We got to bed at about 1 a.m. that morning, hoping that nothing else would happen to call us out.

Lyn Byers, midwife, remote area nurse practitioner and Wendy McNicol, remote area nurse

Christmas Sister
DOOMADGEE, NORTH-WEST QUEENSLAND

'Angry and, at times, intoxicated men can come with weapons seeking their women.' My induction had commenced. 'Lock the doors and drop the front security roller door, if you have time. Then, if you can, exit out the side door; not the back door as others may be waiting. Escape with as many persons as possible to the doctor's residence for safety.'

The voice continued, 'And if a person comes waving a gun, duck down behind the counter and make your escape as best you can.'

'What if I get shot?' I asked, on this my first shift at Doomadgee Hospital.

Point blank, I was told, 'Well, you were just meant to die here!'

'Doom City' was the translation I was given for the Aboriginal word 'Doomadgee'. It was a dry community where some people drank intensely on the other side of the river, then staggered into town bringing violence and aggression with them.

I was told by some, 'If you can nurse here, survive here, then you can nurse anywhere in Australia.' Many persons offered a contract flew in, walked down the steps, looked around and went back on the plane they arrived in.

To me, over time, Doomadgee became the people themselves and a symbol of survival and community against all odds and harsh realities.

At the time I was around, there had been many changes of policies and programs with funding brought in by various 'good' persons. However, just as everything started moving in a certain direction, change was required and it became a case of 'having the rug pulled out from under the feet'. To obtain monies to assist the community, the hope of the community rang through the words, 'We just have to learn to dance on the shifting carpets.'

With the summer rains, the community was isolated, unable to be accessed by road and on many occasions unable to be accessed via air either. I arrived on a small plane for my first Christmas of many to come. Food and even basic medical supplies were very limited for all. There was never any safe drinking water. The children suffered from Third World treatable medical conditions and I soon came to see the differences between town and remote. Senior and discount cards meant nothing here; items seen as rights in the city are unthinkable there.

Assuming they were available, basic treatments and tests performed in the city, without question, had to be justified even for children. Once justified, blood tests which could be stored were collected, spun and sent back with the plane approximately three times a week. Due to the expenses of getting even food in, medical resources were limited and nursing required ingenuity for there were no dressing packs, no ECG machine for heart tracings or ISTAT machines. However, there was a pharmacy and an X-ray machine. I soon learnt as a remote nurse using primary health care guidelines that you had to diagnose, prescribe and dispense plus perform X-rays with limited on-site training. The Royal Flying Doctor Service was a blessing beyond words and the difference between life, death and hope.

Out there, one had very limited choice in food and it was a blessing to have something to eat. A can of spaghetti in the city costing $1 compared to a minimum of $3 at the one store in town and generally there was no fresh food. That first Christmas it was so bleak with limited basic supplies and concern was high for the children, who were showing signs of increasing malnutrition. The elder women worked together to salvage whatever food was available. The children lined up outside on the verandah as the women of the community used the church hall to cook food and serve it to the children. The many hungry adults of the community stood back, going hungry, putting the feeding of the children first. I saw the disease and starvation of Third World countries present here in Australia. My heart broke and my eyes opened.

Except in emergencies when all hands were on deck, we were working minimum twelve-hour shifts with two nurses back to back with two other nurses. We would only call the one available doctor in extremes of life and death.

During another Christmas and New Year period, the town was restless. The hospital wards were full, with weather conditions not allowing the RFDS to land for days.

'Sister, sister. There's a man with a large knife sitting out in the waiting room.'

In the emergency room, when the man with the knife arrived, we were already monitoring the breathing of a male person with a 5-centimetre fish hook embedded in his mouth/throat region, an unconscious woman who overdosed and a male with a neck sliced by a machete that had nicked the carotid artery. Untreated, pulsating blood usually meaning death in a few minutes.

The community had already suffered recent deaths. The crying and gut-wrenching sounds made when a member of community died resonates with me still. We nurses and the doctor were for fighting for the lives of those in the emergency room while monitoring the others. There was no way anyone could move to safety if it was required.

After notifying the police, who were restricted in their ability to respond at that time, I had no choice but to go to the male with the large knife, approaching carefully as he was in distress and could turn it against himself or others at any time.

Fortunately, miracles happen. After several hours had passed, the man handed over the large knife after performing some cuts to his chest and in the nick of time, the RFDS was able to land, retrieving the man with the slash to his neck, the conscious woman recovering from an overdose and the man with the hook in his mouth.

We had been desperately waiting for more staff to arrive, but unfortunately the staff who came to give us some relief returned on the plane they arrived in.

While waiting for still more staff, I was woken from a couple of hours' sleep, called in to assist with a young man wanting to hang himself. There was no other person available and I was studying social work at university. I spent time with this young person and about twelve hours later, he went home speaking about being a role model for other youth in the community.

I became known as 'Christmas Sister', the sister who would, in my uni break, go to Doomadgee to work over the Christmas/New Year period releasing the long-serving nurses for a holiday.

I learnt a new mindset and in the beauty of isolation, learnt to leave behind what I call my 'white mind'. In one Christmas period, Aunty April took me on a walking journey to show me some bush medicines. Aunty April, a respected Aborigine, had a knowing and knew when my time was finally up. That time, Aunty April came to the plane when I was leaving and brought a white handkerchief.

All I saw as the plane took off, and in the air, was Aunty April waving the white handkerchief and eventually, just the white handkerchief; it was my last Doomadgee Christmas.

Kari Richter, registered nurse

Pushed to the Limit

KIMBERLEY REGION, WESTERN AUSTRALIA

Community nursing can be pretty demanding with its 24/7 on-call system for three months at a time, but it can also be very rewarding, where one can forge relationships with the locals on a level that would have no relevance in the world outside. Sharing in the evacuation of an area (due to heavy rains, rising river levels and a proposed 'king tide') by helicopter was indeed an experience that brought out the best and the worst in people.

The helicopters were provided by a nearby off-shore drilling rig and the protocol was to be pregnant women, small children and the elderly first. It was amazing the number of 'older' people who were suddenly quite infirm and the number of women who were suddenly pregnant and who were not willing to risk having their baby on the community, to allow them to have an earlier flight out. Under normal circumstances trying to get heavily pregnant women to go to the nearest big town for 'sit down' and birthing was a constant struggle. Fortunately no-one came to any harm and within days everyone was back (same helicopters) and life returned to normal, apart from a lack of running tap water due to the pump being submerged in the rising waters.

While the pump was being removed and moved to higher ground to prevent a similar situation in the future, bottles of drinking water were flown in for everyday use and 44 gallon drums installed at houses (and the clinic) for washing and toilet-flushing purposes. The 44 gallon drums were filled by a road works water truck at regular intervals and no-one took any harm from the inconvenience.

Being without contact with the outside world was not an uncommon occurrence when the phones were out due to storms or some other interference with the cables. To be on a very isolated community where, during the wet season, the airstrip was out for anything up to three weeks at a time meant using all of one's ingenuity to manage the clinic supplies and to prepare meals at home that were appealing.

Some communities had airstrips that could be used at night for medical emergencies, but flares had to be lit along the boundaries and someone had to drive a vehicle up and down the strip to remove the kangaroos and donkeys so that the plane could land safely. Unless daylight came before it was time to evacuate the patient, the same procedure would have to be repeated for take-off and then the flares brought back in to be safely stored until next time.

On one community I had a middle-of-the-night emergency and with the promise of a plane within the hour, the flares were set up, animals scared off and the patient stabilised for retrieval. Although the patient had suffered a knife injury to his leg that was not life threatening, the knife, which I was not about to try and remove, was still in situ. He was also in a heavy alcohol-induced sleep that lasted until nearly lunchtime, when he eventually surfaced only to be informed that he was still on the community as there had been three attempts at getting a plane in to take him out but, for a variety of legitimate reasons, none had made it.

After two more abortive attempts and with nightfall approaching again, one was finally scheduled to arrive so the setting up of the runway had to proceed all over again. By this time, it was hard to find someone sober enough to help out as some members of the community had been drinking steadily all day. Once the patient was awake and I had adequately shielded the imbedded knife from their curious eyes, he had a steady stream of visitors through and everyone could see he was taking no harm but they still worked themselves into a fury over the repeated delays. By the time the plane arrived the community was near riot point.

To get the patient from the clinic to the plane meant a ride in the back of an open-tray top, and I became aware of the sullen and dangerous atmosphere among some of the local community members who stood along the road as we drove back out to the airfield. We were followed to the airstrip by the community members and, led by a couple of very drunk and abusive people (male and female), a large group stormed the area around the plane where we were attempting to load the patient aboard. The patient's entreaties that he was okay fell on deaf ears and the racist remarks being hurled at us from two people in particular were so out of context with the whole situation that if it hadn't been so serious it would have been funny.

It was not until the pilot refused to continue with the evacuation until the immediate area was clear of all people not authorised to be there that they moved back behind a perimeter fence and allowed the evacuation to take place. By this time, it was fully dark and as the plane taxied to take off, the non-Indigenous community members who had provided the vehicle used to transport the client wanted to leave the area before the situation got completely out of control. However, it was policy that I remain at the strip until the plane was in the air and out of sight, so they drove away and left my husband and I standing beside the clinic vehicle that had accompanied us out there.

I was unnerved by all of this but not really frightened and it was a huge relief when the chairperson's wife left the still-muttering crowd and came stood by me and said, 'Molly, it was not meant to be like this,' and we stood holding hands until the plane was airborne and out of sight. She remained with us until we were safely in our house and left us with the promise that there would be no more disturbances that night.

I had, of course, been in touch with my team leader throughout the day and when I reported this last episode it was decided to pull us off the community at first light. Although I readily agreed, a few hours' sleep (with no callouts) allowed me the space to see that 'running' from such a situation was not the answer to the problem, so, along with the chairperson and his wife, a small group of senior community elders was called and the situation discussed. As there really were only two perpetrators who led the disturbance, I was satisfied that they had been suitably dealt with by their own council members. However, a remark made later in the day to the effect that, had the patient died it would have been Dick and I on the stretchers being taken out, made me realise that 'payback' appeared to be alive and well on this community.

Molly Cobden, registered nurse (remote)

A Tragic Weekend

NORTH-WEST NEW SOUTH WALES

We had been looking forward to the race meeting for months. Pretty dresses and champagne had been sourced weeks before, just for this weekend. This particular race meeting is an annual event in outback NSW where a sleepy little town comes to life, where the population explodes from twenty to 5000. It was only a couple of hundred kilometres away; not so far in the outback.

Very early that Saturday morning, the phone rang.

'We need you at the hospital urgently.' From her voice, I knew something really bad had happened. 'There's been a house fire; two kids are dead.'

I was working in a remote hospital two hours' drive from Broken Hill. When there is an emergency in these small communities, all hands are on deck: to nurse, to make tea, to get notes together, to support your colleagues or do whatever needs to be done. It's not about who's on call; it's about patient care and helping your mates.

In any community the death of a child is devastating. For a nurse in a small remote community where you know the children and their families, it is horrific. I arrived at the hospital to find crowds of people inside and outside the hospital in utter grief and shock.

The grandmother of the children worked at the hospital with us and was much respected and loved. The role of the nurse in this situation is to just be with your grieving community. We are not taking blood pressures or handing out tablets. We hug those that need a hug, make cups of tea, let people cry, talk; just be with them.

When the family, friends and police had gone, we went over to the nurses' home to debrief and grieve together. The camaraderie of colleagues together in grief and shock was most comforting.

While we were still reeling from the death of these children, three nursing colleagues and I all agreed that an outback race meeting and a trip out of town might be good therapy. We headed out late in the morning.

The two-hour drive was an opportunity for the four of us to debrief and cry some more. Playing music in the car also helped. The closer we were to our destination, the more excited we became; it was going to be a good day.

Ten kilometres from the races we came around a bend to see a car on its side, on the side of the dirt road. People were standing around a man lying on the ground, perilously close to the upturned and unstable car. As we pulled up, I recognised one of those standing there; I will call her Sandy. I knew that Sandy had recently become engaged so it wasn't rocket science to conclude that the injured man was in fact her fiancé, whom I will call Aaron.

We jumped out of the car and ran over; Sandy recognised me immediately and told the bystanders to let me help. Before us was a critically ill patient and the nearest hospital was a significant distance away on an appalling road.

In the first aid algorithm, D comes first, D for Danger. The car was on its side and potentially going to land back on the injured patient and on those near him.

The men rolled the car away from Aaron, making it safe to treat him. His injuries were extensive and life-threatening. His airway was severely compromised. Race day was and is the only day of the year that there was an ambulance in this little town, so someone was tasked to go and get help. We had no medical equipment with us.

We had to do something about Aaron's airway immediately. We needed oxygen, suction, IV fluids, and a Guedel airway as a minimum; if we were in any emergency department of any major hospital he would have been intubated, had chest drains inserted and had lifesaving intravenous fluids running. As it was, we didn't have any of those things. We did not have time to wait for the ambulance to come and I wasn't going to sit down and wait, do nothing; things were pretty bad and getting worse.

I had a light-bulb moment. Connected to the windscreen wipers of cars are two small hoses which provide water from a water reservoir under the bonnet to the top of the bonnet. These provide water with which the windscreen is cleaned. While the hoses are not sterile, they are clean. They do not have any residual corrosive or dangerous chemicals like petrol in them; they have only had water in them. So we cut the hoses and used them as an airway. While it did not help Aaron's other injuries, at least he could breathe.

The ambulance arrived and the paramedic gave Aaron IV fluids and oxygen and inserted an airway. A helicopter was said to be in the area and an urgent request was sent out for it. Then we sent a message to the nearest hospital notifying them of Aaron's pending arrival.

Sandy was uninjured and had not left Aaron's side. While

we knew it was a horrific thing for her to watch, there was nowhere we could take her to shield her from this terrible situation. We were on the side of an isolated road with no form of protective structure nearby, not even a tree.

And then Aaron's heart stopped: cardiac arrest. It was awful to be doing CPR (cardio-pulmonary resuscitation) while this young woman, so much in love with her man, pleaded with him to keep fighting to hang on, to stay with her. Finally we got a pulse; the paramedic continued providing ventilation to this very sick man. The helicopter arrived and Aaron was flown out.

As the whirl of the helicopter faded away, we were numb. We had left home gutted by the death of two young children and had then come upon this. We stood almost whispering amongst ourselves, not sure what to do, where to go. Someone said, 'Let's go to the racetrack.' We had lots of our friends there and we needed to be somewhere, doing something.

As we arrived, we could see the police talking to Sandy's parents and we knew that Aaron hadn't made it. We four nurses, who had seen too much for one day, broke down and wept. From out of the crowds around us, some women emerged, whisked us into a private area and allowed us to cry. They hugged us, they comforted us, and they let us grieve. Women in the bush look out for each other. Words could not comfort us in that moment of exhaustion, but the strength and compassion of those women did.

It has been many years since this horrendous weekend. I will always have a great sadness that we lost three good people. However, I will always remember the camaraderie of the nurses on that day, and the compassion of those women who did not shy from others' suffering. They reached out to four distressed women they barely knew, giving us solace and friendship in our time of need. Amidst the tragedy of the weekend, my faith in the human race was strengthened.

Monica Mary Brown, registered nurse

Rollover

BEDOURIE, FAR SOUTH-WEST QUEENSLAND

Several years ago, I was working for Frontier Services at the clinic in Bedourie. Late one Sunday afternoon I got a call from Cluny Station to say they'd had a call on the radio, from a truckie, reporting a bad accident about 80 kilometres east of Bedourie on the Diamantina Developmental Road. The accident site was about 750 kilometres from Charleville and 600 kilometres from Mount Isa so, initially at least, I knew we were on our own. I tried to find the policeman but he was busy elsewhere; consequently, it was the local council mechanic who volunteered to come with me to drive the ambulance and to assist. Having advised the RFDS that I was going out to an unknown scenario, we finally got hold of the policeman to let him know and we headed off.

Calling in at Cluny homestead on the way past, we found they knew little more than the basics first called in. When we got to the accident, we found the truckie waiting, assuring the injured that help was on its way. It was a really nasty single-car rollover involving four young people from one of the stations. One of them had been thrown out so we did a bit of running around the paddock and up the road getting everyone sorted, trying to work out what had happened and, therefore, what their less obvious head, spinal and internal injuries might be. I did consider reverse triage to begin with, sending the case most likely to survive back first, but they were all so badly injured, I decided we needed to get them all back as soon as possible. The young driver had major head injuries and she had developed what's called raccoon eyes and other Battle's signs. They're an indication of brain trauma and I've never seen them develop so quickly.

This was in the days before satellite phones so I had no contact with a doctor or anyone else for that matter. The troopy-cum-ambulance was only equipped for one person so we had limited resources available to manage so many people. We didn't have enough cervical collars; we just managed the best way we could.

In the end, having patched everyone up as well as possible, I commandeered the truckie's semitrailer to help transport the four of them, loading two of the head injuries into his sleeping cab. We loaded one into the back of a ute that had come with us from Cluny and the worst case, a young man with leg deformities and a very boggy pelvis, into the ambulance. He was conscious but I just knew he wasn't well.

I travelled with him and we kept in touch with each other via radio. On the way back, my patient was distressed and uncomfortable and in the confined space of the back of the troopy, he managed to tangle up the IV line so that no fluids were going through. We had to stop, unload the stretcher, sort the IV out and get him stabilised again before proceeding steadily westwards.

Once we got into radio range of Cluny, I was able to get them to call ahead and advise the RFDS that we'd need everything they could send, on the ground, asap. I also got a message to Joyce, the Aboriginal health worker in Bedourie, to get the clinic opened up and ready. Remembering she didn't have keys, when we arrived back at midnight, I was surprised to find the clinic wide open, all the lights on and everything set up. She'd found the bloke who built the clinic and he'd dismantled half the double front door.

It was all hands on deck. Most of the (very small) town appeared to have turned up offering to help and, as I directed them, they helped get all the injured safely into the clinic and as comfortable as possible. Because we didn't have enough beds or trolleys, a couple of them were on mattresses and pillows on the floor. Everyone just did a great job. Joyce took BPs and obs, someone else gently cut off clothes, and every time I looked, the policeman seemed to emptying the rubbish bins . . .

The first RFDS plane arrived from Mount Isa at about 2 a.m. Even the pilot asked how in the hell had we managed to get them all back to Bedourie. A second plane from Charleville arrived shortly after and the doctors decided who was going where. Once the planes were loaded and safely away, we did a basic clean-up and a bit of a debrief then went home and tried to get some sleep.

The community rallied around and supported us by staying away next morning until we got everything in the clinic properly tidied up and ready for the day. I talked to Joyce and the mechanic and the policeman and over the next few days things slowly started to get back to normal. Officially, I never heard anything of the outcomes for the four young victims, but people heard things around the district and let me know that they all survived, although with significant and life-changing injuries.

With time to think about it, I couldn't work out how the young man with the pelvis ended up where he was or how one of the girls managed to crawl into a gap under the upside-down car. And for the life of me, I still don't know how we managed to get them loaded up into the sleeper cab right up in the back of the cabin of the truck. I just know we did exactly what we had to do, with the resources we had, to save their lives.

Over the following days, there were repercussions because I had called Joyce in to help. Her employer in Queensland Health said it wasn't her role, but she did nothing she couldn't do or that I didn't direct her to do. A lot of people just don't understand that when you live and work in a remote area, you make the best possible use of the resources you have.

As a consequence of this experience, I realised that a disaster is not necessarily a cyclone or a bushfire; for a small remote town, a car accident like this is a catastrophic event. I've since got very involved in disaster management so the lessons learnt have been invaluable. In Frontier Services, we have developed strategies for managing multiple injuries should they occur. All of our clinics are better resourced and much better prepared.

Anna Burley, registered nurse

Christmas Every Day

CHRISTMAS ISLAND, TERRITORY OF
AUSTRALIA, INDIAN OCEAN

It's mid-December and a tropical low is developing offshore causing high winds and seas. The supply ship has left again after another unsuccessful attempt to offload essential supplies on Christmas Island. Plumes of sea spray shoot up into the air as waves hit the jetty and surrounding cliff face, and roads are covered in wind-blown debris. As I drive down the cutting, curtains of rain sweep across the point and the sun sends splinters of light onto Flying Fish Cove.

Weather dominates conversation here on this tiny speck in the Indian Ocean as it dictates much of the activity and movement on and off the island. Christmas Island is one of Australia's most remote territories and is situated 2600 kilometres north-west of Perth and 350 kilometres south of Jakarta. The island is a volcanic plug that soars thousands of metres out of the sea bed and is home to a permanent population of around 1500 people. Three-quarters are of Malay, Chinese, Indian or Eurasian descent, with Chinese dialects and Malay the primary languages spoken. The rich cultural heritage is due to a long history of Chinese and Malaysian migration to service the phosphate mining industry over the last one hundred years.

Over the last three years the island's population has swelled due to the influx of asylum seekers and the fly-in-fly-out population employed at the detention centre and the associated service industries. This, along with a rapidly ageing permanent population with a high burden of chronic disease, has provided unique challenges to an isolated health service providing care to a widely disparate group of people. The island had two health services: the Indian Ocean Territories Health Service (IOTHS), which has an eight-bed inpatient facility, and a private health contractor providing initial health induction and ongoing primary health care to asylum seekers in detention.

For the next couple of days, the jetty is closed as 2-metre swells roll in, gouging out the beach and tossing huge logs like twigs. The wind has changed pitch overnight and has gone from a low groan to a keening roar. Next morning there is a low sea mist and driving rain and amongst the howling wind people can be heard yelling, calling; the words can't be discerned but the meaning is clear.

Locals have arrived and are standing along the rocky cliff as a refugee boat has lost power, is pounded by churning surf and is edging dangerously towards the cliff face. People are desperately trying to help by throwing life jackets to the stricken vessel and trying to make human chains, but 3-metre swells and razor-sharp rocks make it almost impossible to do anything until the navy arrives.

A man in the water is trying to keep his head above water but is tiring. He takes a few desperate paddles, goes under and comes up. 'Swiiiiiim!' yell the navy guys. He goes under again and as he comes up is plucked from the churning water. In driving rain, emergency tents are set up at Ethel Beach to receive survivors. Everything and everyone is permeated by the smell of diesel. After initial triage they are transferred to the hospital to be fully assessed. All through the day they come. Some are admitted; some require transfer to the mainland with the RFDS. An emergency morgue is set up.

A man weeps, another woman is inconsolable at the news that her daughter is missing and many are dazed, unable to fathom what has happened. Each survivor has a story. Some have lost their whole family; nobody is unaffected. The media circus starts with phone calls from as far away as Sweden and Iran. A journalist tries to enter the hospital to take pictures of survivors and is intercepted by staff.

As the evening rolls on the RFDS leaves with patients, staff clean and restock, looking for a reason to stay close to others, and then it is time to go. Outside the whole world is exhausted. It is still, no wind, no rain nothing stirs. It seems that all that can be wrenched and laid waste has been.

It's early April and the smell of diesel, faces of the living and the dead, and high winds and seas leave many with a sense of unease. The island's children are still waiting for their Christmas presents to arrive on the supply ship and diesel is running low. Red crabs are crawling up the screen door and out my window I can watch Christmas Island boobies doing aerial dances as they swoop and dive on the updrafts.

It's nearly two years on and a blood red-orange sun sets behind a bank of storm clouds on the Cocos Keeling Islands. Eight asylum-seeker boats are moored in a row in the lagoon. The doldrums have arrived and with it another cyclone season.

Christine Foletti, registered nurse

Highway Patrol

SANDFIRE, NORTH-WEST HIGHWAY,
WESTERN AUSTRALIA

The scene was one of utter carnage. With crumpled bodies lying over the road and verge, the smashed-up hull of a ute gently smoking in a culvert and pools of blood seeping into the red dust, Mick Lanagan went, without hesitation, straight to work.

He raced from casualty to casualty, assessing injuries and working out whose lives he could save and who was just too far gone. The ute had been crowded with people, both front and back, and, driven by an unlicensed minor, had careened off the road and rolled, flinging passengers in every direction. Many were either unconscious or writhing in agony. Even as he was calling on the satellite phone for backup, Mick knew, 270 kilometres south of Broome on Western Australia's Great Northern Highway, it could be a hell of a long time before any other help arrived. Calmly and efficiently, he administered emergency first aid to those he knew stood a chance, tried to stop their bleeding, bandaged their injuries, placed them on their sides and soothed the panicky.

'You have to be a little bit hard sometimes to do triage,' he says. 'But you've got to concentrate on where you can make a difference.' In this case, the volunteer medical worker knew his work could prove critical.

By the time Mick took a breath to look up, five ambulances had arrived at the scene. A Royal Flying Doctor Service

(RFDS) plane had landed on a local airstrip, since it was too windy to attempt to put down on the road, and was ready to airlift patients to Perth.

By then, Mick had been working for a couple of hours in the blistering sun in 47-degree Celsius heat. 'I'd started to feel ill myself, but I hadn't been able to stop,' says Mick, who is diabetic and has chronic back problems. 'But with others on the scene, I slumped down in the shade and a young paramedic came over and said I looked like I should eat something. He gave me a couple of biscuits, which got my blood-sugar level back up again, so I could carry on. I suppose I'd forgotten to look after myself, but I was all right.'

Thanks largely to Mick, who is a resident at the Sandfire Roadhouse halfway between Broome and Port Hedland, just one of the thirteen people in the horror smash was pronounced dead at the scene, and only two died later in hospital. 'You have to be ready for anything when you live in a place like this,' Mick says, sagely. 'The Australian outback can be a tough place, but you have to be prepared for it.'

Mick loves the wide-open spaces of the vast, flat ochre-dust plains that stretch from Sandfire as far as the eye can see, and is eager to help others appreciate its wild beauty. 'I had one young couple call in once who said there was nothing here,' he grins. 'But I told them this is a place you have to look more carefully for the beauty to reveal itself. In one square yard on the ground you can see maybe ten different sorts of little native wildflowers. Then there are so many birds and so much wildlife – although unfortunately a lot of it without legs – it's just incredible. 'And out here, at night, it's so silent you can actually *hear* the stars . . . I can't imagine a better life.'

Along with the beauty, however, comes a fair amount of savagery. The two-lane highway that runs past Sandfire is so dead straight that countless drivers fall asleep at the wheel. That's not to mention the 51-degree Celsius temperatures and the deadly bushfires and fierce cyclones that strike without warning at any time, day or night. People living on stations inland, towards the coast 20 kilometres away, and just about anywhere along the 600-square-kilometre stretch of lonely outback that Mick looks after, all turn to him for help when sickness strikes, accidents happen or someone gets bitten by a snake. He drove 1900 kilometres on a shift once. But as a volunteer for forty-five years with the RFDS and St John Ambulance, Mick always has a safe pair of hands, whatever happens.

'He's unbelievably helpful and his skills are highly regarded,' says Lyle Gilbert, the St John Ambulance station manager at Port Hedland. 'Without him we would certainly have seen a lot worse outcomes, with people having to go a long, long way for help. He started with a genuine concern to help others and he now provides the best care possible for people. He's real salt of the earth, his heart is definitely in the right place and he's a great part of the team.'

By now, Mick's learnt to cope with every kind of emergency, and he says some of his strength comes from being of good, hardy Irish stock. His mum Eileen O'Connor arrived in Australia from Cork as a nine year old with her family and later went to work as a cook and companion on an outback sheep station at Turee Creek, between Paraburdoo and Newman in the Pilbara. There, she met and married George Lanagan, a NSW-born head stockman, and the pair went on to manage a number of remote stations.

George drove cattle four times down the Canning Stock Route and, on his last trip in 1940, thirty-year-old Eileen came along too and, carrying only five possessions – a diary, a pencil, a camera, a gun and a jar of face cream – made history as the only white woman ever to traverse the route with a full mob of cattle. Today, her beautiful black-and-white photos are stored for posterity by the J S Battye Library of West Australian History, an arm of the State Library of Western Australia.

Mick was born in Geraldton in 1946 and was a chip off George's block. By the age of four, with his dad managing Carnegie Station some 500 kilometres east of Wiluna, Mick was riding horses like he'd been born on one, and mustering 500 sheep on his own. Working side by side with his dad, he soon became an expert at running stations, often taking time out going contracting: building fences, installing tanks and putting in windmills.

He fell in love with the RFDS when a stockman was injured and their plane appeared, like an angel, to help.

He tried living in Perth, when his sister Mary fell ill and needed support and help with her kids. But it wasn't for him. 'I hated waking up in the morning, knowing I was in a city,' he says. 'People in the city don't seem to have any manners; they push past you, they're rushing and they're always walking around with their heads down. In the bush, you don't have those kind of routines. You work with the seasons, you fix things when they go wrong, and you're master of your own destiny.'

The only times he returned to the city after that were when he had to be fixed up after station accidents or when, in later years, a battery of tests revealed he had cancer in his spine. Then, after six months in hospital, he discharged himself. 'The place was doing my head in so I decided I'd go back to the outback for some peace and quiet and see how I went there. And I managed to cure myself, with the power of positive thinking. Being out there always helps.'

That kind of mental resilience when the chips are down never fails to impress those who know him best. 'He just willed himself better through sheer determination,' says Meredith Earnshaw, the medical chest officer for the RFDS's Western Operations. 'He makes the best of absolutely everything. He's an old-style bushie, incredibly self-reliant and strong-minded.'

Unable to go back to riding horses, Mick went to join an old mate, Ken Norton, the owner of the roadhouse at Sandfire, who asked him to look after the engines, pumps and lighting plants on the site.

Nestled between the last two monster sand dunes of the Great Sandy Desert, the Sandfire Roadhouse doesn't look too impressive. In 2007, a blaze from an electrical fault roared through the roadhouse, gutting the building and causing $1.5 million worth of damage, and many of the trees that provided shelter to the site were flattened by the ferocious Cyclone Laurence that hit the west coast in December 2009. Everything is now gradually being rebuilt.

Now sixty-three, Mick has become tireless in his devotion to the RFDS and St John Ambulance, and is happy to be the man everyone turns to for help in that part of the world. 'I just love people and it's fun helping,' Mick says. 'Over that 600-kilometre gap between Broome and Port Hedland, they rely on me and my ambulance. It's just a way of life. There's always something that goes wrong in a remote place like this and there's never time to get bored.'

Sue Williams, author and journalist (Mick's story first appeared in Sue's book, Outback Spirit, *in 2010. This edited extract appeared in* RM Williams OUTBACK *magazine in 2011 and appears here courtesy of both Sue and* OUTBACK.*)*

Postscript: Mick was recently forced to retire from driving the ambulance as he is no longer able to manage the stretcher on his own. However, when called, he still goes out in his own vehicle to assist at accidents on the Great Northern Highway. He will triage and treat just as he's always done and provide basic comfort and company to those who wait the long wait for an ambulance to come from Port Headland or Broome and/or the RFDS. He still runs a clinic for the local community, surrounding stations and any passers-by who find themselves in need.

Thank God, Here Comes the Flying Doctor

NORTH-WEST NEW SOUTH WALES

As there was some perception, among the powers that be, that the ambulance was being misused as a taxi service, it was taken off the road for a fortnight and sent away for a service. A station wagon was our backup. There was no room for a trolley, but we called on the SES, should the need to transport patients arise, as they were in possession of a retired ambulance.

On my last work day before going on maternity leave with my first child, a call came through that a truck had rolled about 55 kilometres east of town with one unconscious, one 'real crook', and two walking wounded. Having alerted the Royal Flying Doctor Service (RFDS) that we were going to an accident and the SES that we would need their services with the old ambulance, the Deputy Director of Nursing (DDON), a wardsman, a medical student and I bundled into the wagon and headed east.

Upon arrival we found the unconscious man was deceased. His mate with head, chest and suspected abdominal injuries, as per initial notification, was indeed 'real crook' and there were two walking wounded with no obvious injuries. The pantech had been towing a trailer and, having perhaps gathered speed on the decline, the driver appeared to have lost control and ended up some distance down an embankment.

These four men were a long way from their home in WA and I remember feeling such sorrow for them knowing that it would be some time before they would be reunited with their families, and that one of them would not see his family again. We had no portable radios, so I was going up and down the bank to my colleagues, relaying the doctor's orders as I was getting them over the VHF radio in the car. Not that steep, but somewhat an effort with the load I was carrying.

After a stern instruction from the DDON to say that they were not out on the side of the road to deliver a baby, I was confined mostly to staying with the vehicle. In contact then with the RFDS pilot, I was asked to drive along the highway and find a straight stretch of road for the plane to land.

A few kilometres from the accident scene I found what I thought might be suitable. The only problem was a slight dip at one end. The pilot suggested I drive at 100 kilometres per hour and determine if the car 'bounced' when it hit the dip. *Is he serious*, I wondered? I actually did as requested, slowing down before I became airborne! I reported in that I thought it may still be okay, throwing in all disclaimers of responsibility for my lack of knowledge in construction of airstrips!

Next question from the pilot: did the newfound airstrip run east–west or north–south? In this modern age of mobile phone apps I would have been able to tell him. In their absence, we could both only laugh when I told him the sun was directly above me so I had no idea!

Final test was to take out the guideposts with the bull bar. I thought this was another odd request but the pilot reassured me it was necessary to avoid damage to the plane. *Really?* I wasn't exactly going to argue, being very new to this job description! So I ran over the posts but much to my amazement some sprang back up. On closer examination, they were not the usual wooden ones, but a flexible new design. I'd never seen them before. I had to line them up directly under the tyre to get them to snap off.

I returned to the accident scene where the badly injured patient was stabilised and the walking unwounded had been properly assessed. Some time elapsed and then away in the distance, the first rumbles of the approaching plane whispered over the horizon. As it came into view, I burst into tears. It was the most amazing sight. I was so relieved to see the RFDS and watched in absolute awe the majestic spectacle of this Nomad aircraft soaring above the treetops directly overhead.

We took the patient up to the highway and awaited the landing of the plane. The SES had by this time closed the highway at both ends, and there were many vehicles banked up either side. Some traveller had a video camera and was filming the scene. Poor bugger copped a bit of a mouthful from one very emotional young nurse, upset by the fact he was filming a tragic situation where mates had lost one of their own. I thought it was very insensitive until I turned around, witnessing one of the most memorable days in my nursing career, and wished I'd had a camera too.

Jane Clarke, registered nurse

Somebody's Listening . . .

DOCKER RIVER, NORTHERN TERRITORY

In the autumn of 1975 I was stationed at the small, isolated community of Docker River, a settlement scenically nestled against the Petermann Ranges, 200 kilometres due west of Uluru.

The community had a largely transient population, about 400 people: Pitjantjatjara, Ngaanyatjarra, Yankunytjatjara and Pintubi; all desert peoples who used the fledgling outpost as a convenient staging post as they moved around their traditional countries, at the intersection of the Northern Territory,

South Australia and Western Australia.

A basic services infrastructure was provided by the government. It was delivered via three teachers, two nurses, a shopkeeper, a general maintenance handyman and me, the community advisor.

We lived and worked out of a mixture of odd abodes including a corrugated-iron shed designated as my office, a generator shed and a number of 'silver bullets': large caravans looking something like huge Lego blocks, four kitted out as classrooms, the remainder as staff housing. The store was the community's centrepiece, a solid brick and mortar construction that was actually close to looking like a conventional building. Another corrugated-iron and bush-timbered shed served as the medical clinic. There was a desk and two chairs and a rickety old iron bed as the consultation facility, and the waiting room was a long bench seat on the verandah out the front, as the song goes!

The old Ayers Rock Hotel provided a social outlet and the tortuous four-hour trip, following two wheel ruts between and often over the drifting sand dunes, was considered a small price to pay to occasionally access the 'outside' world. The road had regular use, often three or four vehicles a day. Irregular grading had lowered the track surface several feet below the surrounding levels, a bit like driving in a deep, extended rut. It was a track that required extreme care and attention and definitely not one for the faint-hearted!

Our head nurse, Rae, and her husband declared an intention to spend the weekend at the Boomerang Hotel, at the Rock. As was the custom, they advised me to expect their return on mid-Sunday afternoon. It was duly noted and

I reminded Rae to keep a lookout on the road, as we were expecting the arrival of our fortnightly supply truck sometime over the weekend.

Four o'clock Sunday afternoon came and went. The truck had arrived, unloaded and left at midday for the nine-hour trip back to Alice Springs. At five, our second nursing sister, Pat, came over to my caravan, noting that Rae and her husband hadn't returned. I begrudgingly suggested that they had stayed on for a few extra bevvies, but Pat would not be put off. She returned a few minutes later with the large portable first-aid kit and sent me on my way. I fuelled the Toyota, mumbling about the long trip ahead and thinking about what I would say to the errant couple when I arrived and found them breasting the pub bar.

One hundred kilometres down the track, I came across Rae's husband stumbling along the sandy track. He was mostly incoherent and dehydrated, but managed to tell me that they had hit the supply truck! Another 10 kilometres on, I came upon mayhem: a head-on collision. Rae looked up gratefully, as we pulled up.

Rae had a ruptured patella but for the next ten minutes she hobbled around giving me a comprehensive briefing on the damage. They had offered a lift back to Docker to several local women who had been sitting in the rear of their utility when the accident happened.

I got Rae seated and over the next two hours she closely directed my activities. There was a suspected fractured skull, another compound bone fracture, the two drivers in shock, many cuts and extensive abrasions. Under Rae's supervision I wrapped blankets around the shock victims, gently splinted the break, bandaged a head, applied ointments and success-fully immobilised Rae, who chose this moment to tell me that she was also four months pregnant!

I was working by car headlight now. It must have been about nine o'clock when I thought I heard a car approach-ing. Two minutes later, headlights could be seen bobbing and weaving towards us, from the direction of Uluru. Another two long minutes and four nurses stepped out of their vehi-cle! They were a nursing crew heading out to Warburton, our neighbouring community in Western Australia, another eight hours west.

Coals to Newcastle and a thousand similar thoughts went whizzing through my brain as I quickly did the rounds of our patients with the girls. Satisfying myself that we were now all in good hands, I apparently strolled behind the Toyota and fainted!

The extra vehicle solved the dilemma of how we would get everybody back to Docker. It was squishy, but we got every-one into either the girls' Land Cruiser or into my utility for the slow drive back. We arrived at around midnight with Pat, our ever-vigilant sister, walking into the clinic as we pulled up.

At midnight, the generator had long been switched off. Paraffin tilly lamps lit the scene, casting eerie, elongated shad-ows across the room. While the phalanx of nurses regrouped and worked their wonder, I went across to my 'office' and sought medical support.

In 1975, the RFDS in Alice Springs had a duty officer sleep-ing in the office every night. Outlying settlements and stations were issued with a special two-toned whistle which, theoreti-cally, when blown into the two-way radio, triggered an alarm at the base alerting the duty officer of an emergency. That was the theory! From midnight until 5.30 a.m., we whistled, three seconds on the long whistle, two seconds on the short. God I hated that device.

As dawn approached, a deep Texan drawl came over my radio.

'Who in hell is making all that squawkin' racket?'

A brief pause of bewilderment and disbelief as I replied, 'Ah, hello.'

'Yep, who are you guys makin' that god-awful noise?'

Relief started to flood through my system. 'Ah, g'day, I am at Docker River and we have a medical emergency.'

'Goddam, where on this good earth is Docker River?'

'In Central Australia,' I replied. 'Look, I don't have their number but could you get it and phone the Royal Flying Doctor Service in Alice Springs and get them to come to the radio?'

While we waited about five minutes for the RFDS duty officer to come on the line, our Texan saviour advised that he was in a US military transport approaching Guam!

The RFDS plane arrived at about nine o'clock that morning and all patients were air-lifted in to Alice. Our tired, extended crew drew breath as the Warburton-bound nurses radioed Warbo' advising that they would be a day late. They then threw their swags under my caravan and had a breather as the community got on with another day.

I have often pondered the wonders of technology; Guam, but not Alice! I never did think to ask for the guy's name, nor that of the nurses, but belatedly, a grateful thank-you for your collective efforts on that night so long ago!

In due course all evacuees recovered and returned to Docker, and Rae's baby arrived fit and healthy several months later.

Chris Burchett, former community advisor

chapter five

WINGING TO WORK

Sometimes the only way to get to work is on a plane . . .

Night Flight to Wyndham

DARWIN, NORTHERN TERRITORY/
WYNDHAM, WESTERN AUSTRALIA

It's 2 a.m. and we are on our way from Darwin to the little muddy port of Wyndham, in northern Western Australia, to pick up a stockman who's come off second best with a pair of hooves and whose condition is deteriorating.

The Aerial Medical doctors would normally have done the flight but they have flown their maximum hours and the flight nurses have a bug so the Medical Dove is grounded. I am a casualty nurse at Darwin Hospital. That's why I'm sitting alone in the cabin of a Mickey Mouse Airlines (MacRobertson Miller Airlines) DC3 staring out into the darkness . . .

I remember back to my first week at the Darwin Hospital. I'd spent two days working in, and familiarising myself with, casualty, then found myself on night duty. Just me, on my own, with a doctor on call. The first thing I had to get acquainted with was the night switchboard, which sat behind the door in the sisters' office. It was a funny old contraption of levers and flaps and I needed to be able to make and take calls on the run. Above the switchboard the air-crash manual demonstrated its importance by hanging from its own hook. Someone had told me I was to read this manual when I had time. 'No rush, mind. There's never been an alert that anyone can recall.'

My first night shift went well. The first patient was a rather scruffy man with half a bottle of port in his coat pocket and a dead snake in a brown paper bag. He'd been bitten, he said, and showed me the tourniquet above his knee. I took his obs, which were normal, and looked in vain for fang marks. He had been sleeping rough and was covered with scratches and cuts. His obs remained normal.

I looked at the snake and read up about identification and antivenom. There was a huge amount of information. Some of it, such as the ribbon-like information pamphlets accompanying the antivenom, was so huge it'd been printed in tiny letters and needed a magnifying glass to read it.

A second patient arrived. Did I have anything to cure a hangover? I gave him a couple of aspirin and asked if he knew anything about snakes. As luck would have it, he used to work with the Wildlife Department. I showed him the snake and he became almost rapturous with delight. It was a something-or-other python and appeared to mean a great deal to him. The fact that it was not venomous meant a lot to me and would, I suspect, have meant even more to the bloke in the coat.

With his hangover overtaken by having fun with snakes, he gave me a quick lesson in jaws, retractable fangs, anal scales and a few other identifiers. My snakebite patient snored quietly. His obs stayed normal. Probably all he wanted was a bed. So the night passed . . .

One of the pilots comes out of the cockpit and asks if I would mind playing hostess and make a pot of tea. 'Have a bit of a poke around,' he adds. 'They usually give us something to munch on.' He shouts this, of course. A DC3 might be fun, but it's very noisy.

Down the back of the cabin there is a hot-water urn simmering away, loose tea in a caddy, a sugar bowl and a slab of juicy fruitcake in a tin. China cups too. While the tea is brewing I peer out the window. In the distance a storm is lighting up the clouds. Below, it's pitch black.

I've been to Wyndham before; people say it's a shabby little town but I like it just the way it is. We start losing height and beneath us, I can see just two lights. We begin circling. Round and round. Round and round. I flew in here ten days ago and we didn't circle like this. I don't think we circled at all. I start to wonder if something is amiss; the landing gear for instance?

Just before dawn on my third shift of night duty, I had taken possession of a deadly stonefish. It was in a bucket of sea water and still very much alive and the man who presented it to me had been celebrating something – possibly the stonefish – for some hours.

I asked why he was giving it to me. He staggered a little then used his eyes to direct my attention to the top of a cupboard where ancient specimens of box jellyfish, red-back spiders, various snakes, one blue-ringed octopus and several stonefish floated listlessly in jars of murky, yellowing formalin. Considering the state he was in, I figured if I didn't take it he just might be my next patient.

Before I could tell him the good news the air was filled with a wail that split the night and pretty much sobered Stonefish Man on the spot. I traced the horrific noise to the switchboard, where a little metal flap I had not noticed before had flopped down to reveal three words: Air Crash Alert.

I tried to close the flap to stop the noise so I could think, but it wouldn't stay closed. I grabbed the (as yet unread) air-crash manual folder from its hook and ripped open the cover. There in huge red letters spread diagonally down the page was written: 'PANIC!!!'

At that moment the wailing stopped and sanity returned. The phone rang. At least I was on firm ground here. I flipped the lever. It was the airport wondering why I hadn't answered the alert. A voice calmly told me that the Medical Dove with two crew and three passengers was coming in from Snake Bay on Melville Island and they feared the landing gear hadn't locked down. I was to implement the procedures in the manual and was given the ETA, which was not far off considering the landing gear had already been lowered.

The instructions in the manual were clear and easy to follow. The first thing I had to do was alert our two ambulance drivers and the second was to get two trained, off-duty nurses to go to the airport with the ambulances. Then I had to call the doctors, the matron, the medical superintendent, the on-call laboratory technician, the police, the mayor and the Administrator for the Northern Territory, etc. After that I had to call in all the off-duty nurses.

I rang for the on-duty ambulance driver. It took time for me to convince him I was not playing games. He promised to try to find a second driver. There were two phones in the nurses' home, one on each floor. No-one answered either of them. I kept ringing and finally a sleepy voice mumbled, 'Hello?' I explained the situation and said I needed her and another nurse to get dressed immediately and go with the ambulances to the airport.

She laughed, gurgling, 'I'm not falling for this,' and hung up! The airport rang. 'Where are the ambulances?' I rang Matron. She told me to call the medical superintendent. One doctor, the one who wasn't on call, came in. Oh wonders to behold.

In the meantime I went over to the nurses' home and banged on doors. With some persuasion, two of the nurses finally took off for the airport, one of them driving the second ambulance. The plane landed safely, its landing gear firmly locked in place. A faulty indicator light was the diagnosis.

At the end of the shift I found the stonefish still in its bucket of salt water. A large metal tray had been placed on top with two bricks holding it down. What a nice gift for the day staff . . .

The plane banks. I can see a few more lights and soon we're safely on the ground at Wyndham. It's a quick turnaround. Just time to say 'hi' to the nurse and get an update on the patient's condition while the stretcher is secured in the cabin. Soon we're up in the air again and heading north-east.

The stockman had some morphine and is sleepy. The horse kicked him in the back and there appears to be some kidney damage but no-one is sure how bad it is. His obs are reasonable considering. While he is asleep, I play hostess again and make the tea.

The stars are huge against the dark sky and there is a pale gleam on the eastern horizon. Piccaninny daylight. Later comes the true dawn with a molten sky ahead and away to the west the soft clouds are painted orange and pink and lavender. The cabin is filled with the most beautiful light. Down below is the dark, lacy outline of the mangrove-lined coast.

We begin the descent into Darwin and the changing pressure wakes the man. He turns his head towards the window. 'Geez, will ya look at that,' he says drowsily. 'Isn't that something?'

Margaret Hanlon Dunn, retired registered nurse

Offshore Nurse

WANDOO B OIL PLATFORM, INDIAN OCEAN

I'd been working in a regional hospital for several years and volunteering as an ambulance officer when a friend started regaling me with stories of life working as a medic on an oil platform. The idea appealed so I put myself through the Tropical Basic Offshore Safety Induction Emergency Training (TBOSIET), as well as Helicopter Landing Officer and Industrial Medic courses. Then I resigned from my permanent job and worked casual shifts so that I'd be free to take off at short notice.

I got my break on the Wandoo B oil platform in 2008. Located 80 kilometres north of Dampier, it was my first time offshore and a real eye-opener! Flying in to the production platform on a helo was no drama as I had been in the army for nine years. The thing that impressed me most was the sheer size and cleanliness of the platform and the variety of marine life living around this artificial reef.

An oil rig is a drilling rig with a large derrick for drilling oil and gas wells. Wandoo B is a production platform which pumps oil up from reservoirs underneath the seabed and then processes it before pumping it into storage prior to export.

The other significant impression I gained on that first flight in was the potential for injury. I'm working 80 kilometres from the nearest hospital and the only access is via helicopter; if anything needs to be done it's up to me to do it. I realised my skillset would need upgrading. I started attending courses at Royal Perth and Fremantle hospitals before I heard about the health organisation CRANA*plus*. Through them I have undertaken several courses in First Line Emergency Care (FLEC) and with support from my employers at Wandoo B, I attended a Remote Emergency Care course in Broome in 2010, and was stoked at the skills I picked up. Recognising the benefits, my employer has made the FLEC training mandatory for all their offshore nurses.

Getting to work means a two-hour drive from Bunbury to Perth then a two-hour flight to Karratha. There I board the helo for the twenty-minute flight out to the platform. On disembarking the helicopter, I hand my lifejacket to my back-to-back (the medic who's on while I'm off) and start work as the helicopter landing officer (HLO) in charge of the helideck. The next two weeks is very much *Groundhog Day* as I settle into the routine of life offshore.

As well as being the HLO, my role includes being the remote area nurse, logistics administrator and radio operator.

At safety meetings, I'll often give a health presentation. These tend to be driven by what's topical at the time, either in the media or for the crew and their families. Then there's the odd other job the field superintendent handballs to me.

My official day starts at 0600 hours and goes through to 1800 hours, but I'm also on call at night. We have a toolbox meeting every day at 0600 and 1745. For serious accidents I have access to an aero medical evacuation team based in Karratha, who can get to the platform quickly, if they're available, otherwise as soon as possible. In the meantime, it's my job to stabilise the patient and prepare them for transport.

Routine and discipline are important factors of life on the platform and we live, for the fifteen days of each hitch, in an all-male environment. That's fine – we all use 'man logic' – we just can't find anything! The platform has multiple levels and no lifts so everyone gets plenty of exercise. We also have two gyms, indoor and outdoor, and all rooms have wi-fi, TV and a DVD player. The marine environment surrounding the platform is incredibly diverse and a source of continuous interest. We are constantly surrounded by turtles, sea snakes, fish of all shapes and sizes and heaps of really big sharks. I've seen manta rays and whale sharks and best of all, we get the annual migration of humpbacks.

Nursing offshore really is living the dream.

Stephen Fuller, registered nurse

Out on the Wing

ALICE SPRINGS, NORTHERN TERRITORY

A few years ago, we were on a routine RFDS clinic run, taking an ophthalmology (eyes) registrar and an ophthalmology nurse up to Ti Tree, when we get a call on the radio from the comms officer (communication officer) back at base. He said, 'Judy, you better hang around Ti Tree, you might get a bit of trade.' From the way the message was passed through, I assumed that the person didn't have severe injuries; how wrong I was.

So we continue on up; it's only a forty-minute flight from Alice Springs. We land and taxi in to the gate where we're met by the remote area nurse (RAN) hobbling.

'What happened to you?' I asked.

'We've got road accident. I fell down a pothole trying to get this bloke out of the car. We've got him back at the clinic but he's unconscious, there's lots of blood around and he's in a very bad way.'

We get into the clinic and this guy's very obviously not good. The RAN was still hopping about, but her two colleagues were ex-ICU (intensive care) nurses so between us all, we had plenty of expertise.

'Right,' I said to the registrar, 'can you intubate him?'

But no, she didn't think she could do that and then the pilot, looking a little pale, said, 'Judy, I really don't like the sight of blood.'

'That's all right,' I said, 'I don't expect you to look but I do need you to be gopher. I need a couple of pieces of equipment from the aircraft and can you ensure everything is ready so that we can load and go?' So off he goes and next thing he comes back and he's crabbing sideways around the edge of the door with his arm outstretched, looking away from the man and the blood, with this bag dangling off his finger. 'Craig, just throw it in!'

Meantime, I rang the on-call doctor back at Alice who initially told me to just load him in the plane and bring him back. However, part of our job as flight nurses on the ground is ensuring the doctor has a clear picture of the situation, so I said, 'We can't just load him. His airway's insecure; every time we move him he vomits.'

The doctor gave us the go-ahead to intubate him, so between us we got him stabilised and ready for flight. After a quick assessment of the RAN, we decided to take her too as she thought she had a broken bone in her foot.

Leaving the ophthalmologist to get on with her clinic, we took off. Unfortunately, although we got him back to hospital in Alice, from whence he was transferred to Adelaide, ultimately the guy didn't make it. But at least between us we got him home to South Australia and his family got to say goodbye to him. For us, that was something. The thing is, it's all about teamwork: everyone pitching in and doing their job or whatever is needed of them.

The weather is a challenge because we're not working in the controlled climate of a hospital. We can be out there in blistering heat or freezing cold and rain and of course sometimes the weather dictates whether we can fly at all. Working in the confined space of an aircraft can be difficult but you adapt to meet the challenge.

Technically, we work twelve-hour shifts with twelve hours off. Sometimes it can be longer because you have to get back from wherever you are. The duty doctor tasks the plane. That means he/she takes the initial call and does the triage (prioritises severity and therefore order of treatment). We always do a pre-flight assessment so that we can get a comprehensive handover of the patient's condition; this will also determine if we need additional equipment or if the flight nurse feels they need a doctor on the flight. If the nurse is concerned, the doctor has to fly but most flights don't have a doctor on them.

Lots of people are scared of flying. When we do retrievals or evacuations, if we're able to or if it's really needed, relatives come too. You often have to chat and even joke with the patients and/or rellies during the flight. Sometimes they are terrified, not just of the flight but of the whole scenario and keeping them engaged is part of our job even as we're working.

I always tell them that the most dangerous part of the journey is the ambulance ride to the strip because there are fewer idiots up in the air!

Occasionally, I've been caught out. Once we were on an inter-hospital transfer flying a man to Adelaide from Broken Hill and when speaking with his wife, who was desperate to accompany her husband, she revealed she was very scared of flying; my instinct was not to take her with us. However, we decided after much deliberation to take her along. When we got on board I explained all the sounds she would hear and how everything worked and what the safety procedures were. So, we took off and I just kept chatting to her and we were going along okay then, suddenly, we hit an almighty bump.

Next thing the oxygen mask dropped down from the ceiling and she screamed . . .

Oh my God! I thought. To her, I quickly and very firmly said, 'I forgot to tell you that sometimes, on this plane, the mask falls down when we hit a bump! We're okay! There's nothing wrong!' I finally got her calmed down, reminding her that her husband was the sick one. We eventually got to Adelaide but I later reflected that I should always follow my initial gut instincts.

There is a strong connection between people who work for RFDS. Our success is based on teamwork and the belief that no-one is any more or less important than anyone else. We need everyone to ensure good outcomes. The engineers keep the planes in the air, the pilots fly them, the doctors contribute their skills and knowledge, as do the flight nurses, and the communications staff make all the connections. While the flight nurses obviously aren't doctors, we do have certain advanced skills and responsibilities. You certainly can't afford to be a prima donna. At the end of the day, we all need to work together.

I love my current role as nurse manager for South Eastern Section. I like the responsibility and autonomy and that I still get to do clinical work when I relieve staff. This section has bases at Broken Hill, Dubbo and Essendon in Melbourne, where we operate a NEPTS – Non-Emergency Patient Transfer Service – and we have full-time staff at Moomba and Ballera in the Cooper Basin oil and gas fields who undertake both primary health and emergency roles. The section is a big area with diverse people, geography and challenges.

Most people, especially nurses, stay with RFDS for a very

long time. The organisation prides itself on appointing the best person for the job and we have some extraordinary people working for us. For instance, Chris Belshaw was the first nurse practitioner in the RFDS in Australia. He's the team leader in the Cooper Basin based at Moomba. He grew up in Belfast during the troubles and he tells a story about wanting to join the army, but his father told him he thought that was probably a poor career choice in Northern Ireland! Instead he trained as a nurse in Belfast and then England. The scope of his training and experience and how he came to be working for us is a story just on its own.

People will often remark how exciting our jobs must be but, while we certainly can have our share of excitement, it is not all high-end drama. We have some quite routine flights which can also be great; just having the time to chat and hear a patient's story or witnessing a patient's excitement about returning to their home town after receiving treatment in a city hospital away from their family and friends is satisfying.

If there *is* an emergency, for the staff or people waiting for us on the ground, hearing the aircraft flying over is said to be such a relief.

As a team, we all know we're contributing to the health and wellbeing of the people who live, work or travel in the outback and that's a pretty good thought to take home at the end of the day.

Judy Whitehead, nurse manager, South Eastern Section, RFDS

Pormpuraaw Dreaming

WEST CAPE YORK, NORTH QUEENSLAND

I'm a clinic nurse based in Cairns with the Royal Flying Doctor Service. I was in Charleville for five years when I first joined the Service then five and a half years ago, I moved to Cairns. I was on the evac and primary health care teams when I first came up here but for the last five years, I've been doing primary health care clinics at Pormpuraaw, which is a fishing community located just south of Weipa on the western coast of Cape York. In the first couple of years I also did the western clinic run; these clinics included Georgetown, Einasleigh, Mount Surprise, Forsayth and Croydon.

Each week, I fly over to Pormpuraaw for three days so I basically have two lives: my Pormpuraaw life and my Cairns life. Pormpuraaw has about 650 residents plus people in the fishing camps and on properties, some of whom aren't Indigenous. It takes about two hours to fly to Pormpuraaw in a Cessna C208 (Caravan) and I stay Tuesday and Wednesday nights, which gives me an opportunity to do some extra education with the community. I might have a video night or a girls' night or run Core of Life program.

Sometimes I do other clinic runs on other days of the week, to Croydon for instance, or Chillagoe. It's a dream job, the best in the world. I do some emergency clinical work when in community though there are remote area nurses based there with Queensland Health, so I only need to help in an emergency if the clinic does not have enough staff on the ground.

Mostly I undertake primary health care, including health promotion. I do a lot of child health and immunisations. The child health includes treatment of skin conditions, ear infections and anaemia, and completing child health checks, including keeping hearing screening up to date. The RFDS nurse has the endorsement that allows us to treat and then supply medications for these conditions.

Pormpuraaw is a happy, relatively healthy, self-managed community. There is a canteen at the football club. They have a football team and it's a very active and well-run club. Grog is banned out in the community and there is a limit to the amount of drinks you can buy at the canteen. Patrons are breath-tested on arrival and if they're not zero blood alcohol, they are not served and as it means they must have sly grog, they may be reported to the police. Everyone has a Pormpuraaw Football Club card that is swiped with each drink bought. When the limit is reached, that's it, no more. You can't buy takeaways. It was the community's decision and they manage the club and the canteen.

The school retention rate is pretty good although it can always be better. The personalities of the staff sometimes has an impact on retention levels. Someone in the community is responsible for getting older children organised to attend boarding school, as Pormpuraaw School goes to Grade 7. The children go away to Cairns, Rockhampton, Brisbane, Herberton, Ingham and Toowoomba schools. One of my roles is making sure the children have bodies and relationships education before they go away. I run Core of Life a couple of times a year for the children twelve years and above. This program teaches the adolescents the skills that they need to make lifestyle decisions, you know, educated choices about whether they want to be pregnant or not, and learning to budget so they know the cost of having a baby. One of the girls who finished Senior is off in Cairns doing her enrolled nursing at TAFE, which is a great outcome. She is doing well.

I have been running a program every Thursday for three years with the preps and pre-preps called Crocodile Kids. This is an early literacy program (singing songs, rhymes with Indigenous focus) and also encourages the children to care for each other. I also read a book with a health message. The book could be about lying, worries, protective behaviours or acceptance of each other. This program also builds relationships with the education staff, health staff, children and families.

The Circle of Security Parenting Program is making an impact. Generations ahead will see a difference. This is a parenting program based on attachment and is being well received.

Currently, I have four anaemic kids out of roughly 150. That's great. Their ears and eyes are good though dental care is still a challenge. Apart from the lack of available dentists, parents want to please their kids so they buy them lollies. Consequently dental health is suffering. We do have dental care programs happening at school and one-on-one education is provided in the child health room, but it is a problem still.

Another issue that could be minimised is gambling. Card games are popular and are very social. I would like people to have more education around budgeting so that they have their gambling money and enough money to buy food for their families. When the tax cheques come in gambling is huge; thousands of dollars can be in the ring. Some people don't go to work then – instead they stay home and gamble. There's not much in the way of hard drug use in the community but some people do smoke gunja (marijuana) and that can cause mental health problems, particularly schizophrenia. There's a high incidence of mental health problems running in some families.

It's still the best job in the world though. I love working for RFDS because you have so much autonomy to get on and do the best job you can. If the funding was cut or Pormpuraaw didn't need me any more I'd go out and take up remote area nursing, but while they'll have me I'll stay here.

The kids at Pormpuraaw call me Nana, Aunty, big mooki or Miss Lisa. When they leave the room I often say 'love you'. The mothers and children now say 'love you'. Hopefully my time here will add to the children's great memories of their childhood.

Lisa Smith, registered nurse

The Airstrip Clinic
WEST KIMBERLEY REGION,
WESTERN AUSTRALIA

We did all the maternity and antenatal assessments on our RFDS clinic runs. At one station, there were probably five or six house girls who were pregnant at the same time. We didn't go into the homestead for cups of tea, so we did everything under the wing of the plane on the airstrip. I gave out the little yellow-topped bottles to get a wee specimen, but it took so long because the ladies had to find a bush and then they'd have all the petticoats. The skirts and the petticoats would come up and eventually you might get the specimen.

So I thought, *Well, I'll streamline this. I'll give them all a bottle and when they hear us coming next time they'll have the 'speci' ready when we arrive.* I'd never ever said piss or shit in my life, but I had to because this was the language that was used. I couldn't say to them, 'I'd like a urine specimen in this bottle.' So I said to them all, 'Every time when that Flying Doctor plane comes, now you piss in your bottle and bring them up to me.'

We only used to go there for clinic once a month and I'd forgotten that other planes came to the station. Anyway, in the end, the Flying Doctor plane did land, but it wasn't our clinic flight; it was Mr Holman and Sister Camille doing the leprosy survey. Mr Holman came back that evening and said, 'I don't know what you want them for, Doll, but I've got six specimens of piss here for you!'

Apparently it created a bit of a disruption to the household. The manager was quite cross in the end; every time the pregnant house girls heard a plane, they downed tools, raced off to piss in their bottles and then ran them up to the airstrip.

Adapted from 'The Airstrip' by Dasee Gugeri, RN, RFDS Derby, 1967–69 courtesy of the Kimberley Nurses History Group publication, Boughsheds, Boabs and Bandages: Stories of Nursing in the Kimberley

chapter six

ANIMAL TALES

*Called upon to deal with whatever turns up, nurses in
rural and remote areas often serve as proxy veterinarians,
but sometimes the animals in their lives are more of a
threat than a challenge.*

It's Not Easy Being the Vet

BIRDSVILLE/BEDOURIE, FAR SOUTH-WEST QUEENSLAND

Australian Inland Mission nurses never refused treatment to one of God's creatures in trouble, which often got us into sticky situations dealing with animals. Knowing as much about veterinary work as I did about brain surgery (which amounted to zero), I still couldn't turn away an animal in distress if I could help it.

While sitting quietly in front of the big white screen waiting for the weekly movie to start rolling, I was called to treat a de-pelted dog that had skinned its back on corrugated-iron sheeting. After reviewing the upset canine in its owner's backyard, I directed them to bring the cantankerous mutt to the hospital for wound suturing. Under the fluorescent lighting the open wound glistened and the roll of skin and fur gathered near his tail could be pulled back into place and stitched together. As Butch had the reputation of biting anything that moved, I gave him a sedative injection before I started sewing him up as I didn't intend to become a casualty. Once he was adequately sedated and muzzled, I pulled his pelt back into position and sewed it together with catgut sutures that would dissolve in time and not require removal.

Months later I went up to Bedourie to provide medical cover for the racing carnival and carried a small supply of various narcotic drugs in my shirt pocket in case there was a fall. In my wildest dreams I couldn't have envisaged being asked to use the strong pain-relieving drugs on a horse. The race meet was a big social gathering for the locals and I enjoyed catching up with folk I hadn't seen in ages. The nags galloped around the track to the cheers of the locals who had a bet on, while the rest of us gathered at the rail.

It was during the second-last race that a prize-winning mare suddenly came to a stop in the middle of the track and the jockey jumped off her back after hearing a loud crack. He thought she must have broken her leg as she became very distressed and limped off the track favouring her front leg. My knowledge of equine anatomy amounted to zilch so I didn't offer my services.

Halfway through the last race I felt a tap on my shoulder and turned to see the concerned racehorse owner who asked if I was carrying any pain medication that I could give his distressed mare. With my brain in overdrive I contemplated what to give a horse as I made my way to the stalls, and the equine gods guided my hovering hand as I checked my cache of narcotics. For no other reason than it felt right, I decided to give the two ampoules of morphine and not one of the synthetic drugs I had with me. Returning home that evening, I had to enter the horse's name in the drug book to account for the two missing morphine ampoules.

Once the mare was a little more settled she was loaded on the horse float and taken home. Later that evening a vet from the city flew in by charter plane to treat the expensive racehorse and diagnosed a fractured sesamoid bone in the fetlock, which usually meant putting the animal down. The owners wanted to give her every chance of recovery, so kept her in the home paddock for weeks until it became clear that her racing days were over. The mare then took on the role of foster mum for the new foals and spent her days grazing in the nearby fields.

During one of the Flying Doctor visits a month or so later I mentioned that I'd had to treat a horse, and he mentioned that the animal may have collapsed if I'd given it synthetic drugs. That was a close call as I'd been undecided what to give it and may have ended up with a dead horse.

Sue Nilon, retired registered nurse

Bush Vet
NORTHERN TERRITORY

I should have known when I decided in 1993 to go bush, I was probably going to be in for a few surprises. I was advised by a few of my friends already working in the Northern Territory that if I was going to work in remote communities I should practise up on my suturing skills. So I began to practise suturing on a piece of pickled pork. This I am told is the closest thing to human skin and tissue.

I was sent off to a remote community north-east of Alice Springs for my introduction to bush nursing. I was very excited and couldn't wait to commence working in the clinic the next day. However, when my friends waved goodbye I was very much beginning to feel the apprehension settle.

It was only a few minutes later that one of the community members came to my door saying there had been an accident and could I go with her to the patient? The patient turned out to be a young female dog who had given birth recently to a litter of pups. The problem was she'd been involved in an accident and her teats were hanging off. My enthusiasm by this stage was waning. Never mind, I thought, I can really practise my newly acquired suturing skills. I was hoping to appear very in control, though one look at my face would have given the game away.

I reassured my doggy patient, cleansed the injury site as directed by my CARPA Standard Treatment Manual and my friend's recent instructions, and went about suturing the new mother's teats back into pretty much the same place as where they had been earlier in the day. I was so happy to see in the next few days both mother and her babies all feeding naturally.

I have very many happy memories of my time in the Northern Territory and have been very privileged to work with other bush nurses, Aboriginal health workers and all the wonderful resilient Aboriginal people I was proud to have met.

Jennifer Bailey, registered nurse

My Hero

SOUTH AUSTRALIAN/WESTERN AUSTRALIAN
BORDER COUNTRY

Years ago I went out to a station that sits just over the SA–WA border on the only hill for hundreds of miles around. I went there to be governess for the friend of a friend I'd done midwifery with. As the station was also the local bush nursing centre (a caravan) and weather reporting station, I ended up doing all sorts of other things.

The only other building was a motel-cum-café/bar, refuelling stop with a small landing strip down near the sand dunes, catty-corner across the highway. At that time the bitumen stopped at the border, a few kilometres back. They were in the process of building a BP service station right on the border, which was completed while I was there. I actually added cleaner to my jobs, while they were building, as there was no-one else to do it.

As the owners of the station were unable to get away together, because of the above commitments, they viewed my arrival with open arms, and promptly decided to take advantage by taking several holidays in Perth. There are many tales to tell, humorous and horrendous, of my time out there, but this one particularly sticks in my memory.

We occasionally got messages via the radio about escaped convicts from Perth, possibly heading across the Nullarbor to try and lose themselves in an eastern city. We also had a young policeman who spent most of his time off fishing, who was supposed to be available to back me up in times of trouble. I had a white German shepherd, Sabre by name, who was the love of my life at the time and much more effectual than the policeman.

A call came in, mostly put to the back of my mind as I was busy at the time, but when a seedy, burnt young man appeared walking up my hill, the alarm bells rang. The story he gave, of being burnt when he took off his radiator cap, was vaguely believable. I did get a lot of rough-looking types turn up on my doorstep; the fettlers from Reid and the fishermen from Madura (a volatile mix, with alcohol, occasioning some extensive patch-ups), but this guy made me uneasy. I put him in the 'hospital' caravan and nervously attempted to chat. I took Sabre in with me as I started to peel some debris from the second-degree burns.

He smelt heavily of alcohol, but I offered him pain relief, which he (very suspiciously) refused. I must admit to disappointment as I was contemplating some heavy-duty sedation to make him amenable while I went inside and phoned the motel for help. I reiterated that it would hurt as it was obviously not a recent burn and was already infected; it needed to be cleaned. He refused to let me call the Flying Doctor and told me to get on with it. I tried not to ask too many probing questions, like where was his vehicle? I hoped the alcohol in his system would aid the pain relief and he would leave promptly.

Despite my caution, unsurprisingly he was agitated. He suddenly started screaming abuse at me and tried to grab me forcibly around the throat. At this, my Sabre leapt from the floor and launched his 54 kilos at *his* throat. Luckily for him he had his arm raised, and Sabre only ripped the arm and not his throat. My hero did sit on him though, holding the arm and snarling meaningfully, while I rather shakily said, 'Good boy, hold!' as though he was a trained attack dog and not my big, sooky mate!

I dashed across to the house to phone the motel where, needless to say, the policeman was unavailable. However, four fishermen were drinking in the bar. They came and rescued me, staying while I gave him a heavy dose of Largactil and rather ineptly sewed his arm up.

It turned out he really was a nasty piece of work who could have easily done me major damage or even killed me, if it hadn't been for Sabre, my hero.

Julie Hogarth, registered nurse

Good Neighbours

YARAKA, CENTRAL WESTERN QUEENSLAND

I first met Janine Hawkes ('Neen' as she was known) in March 1994. She was the district nurse in the Yaraka area. I had moved up from a property near Quilpie to manage Mount Marlow. Neen and her husband John (known as Hawkes) owned a small property called Merrigal, adjoining Mount Marlow. Neen's a born nurse and became a godsend to me over the next seven years, culminating in saving my life. Many were the times she stitched up my dogs and me after various station accidents.

My first experience of Neen's expert nursing care was when I first arrived at Mount Marlow. I had stitches in my arm, which she removed for me. She always seemed to be stitching up my left hand: cuts from the slip of a knife when killing sheep and cattle for meat for the station. Occasionally she used to take charge of the Isisford Hospital, and after a few trips to Isisford to repair another cut, my wife bought me a mesh glove for that hand.

I was pumping up a truck tyre at Mount Marlow once, when the split rim flew off and hit me in the forehead. The result was another 35-kilometre trip to Merrigal for stitches. Another time I can remember lying on the lounge-room floor at Merrigal while Neen did another repair job, with one of her small daughters holding my hand and offering me heaps of comforting words!

I ran a chainsaw into my leg on another occasion; the list seems endless. Neen was always removing Mulga sticks from our legs, a consequence of mustering on motorbikes. If it wasn't sticks, it'd be metal or some such thing from our eyes.

Many of my dogs were repaired by Neen on the floor at Merrigal. Two cases spring to mind. The first was when one of my dogs was racing down beside a weldmesh fence. There was one piece of weldmesh which had broken off one end, and was sticking out. The dog ran it up his hip, causing a long, deep cut, which Neen stitched up for me. The other time I was out on a bike running waters, not long after shearing. I noticed one woolly sheep running with all the freshly shorn ones. I cut him out of the mob and told the dog to go and catch it for me. He jumped off the bike, and strangely pulled up, sat down and looked at me. I said, 'Go on, get hold of him.' He caught the sheep but when I rode over to them I noticed there was blood just pouring out of his foot. On closer inspection I found that he had torn one of his claws and pad off his back foot. I still have no idea how it happened, and can only guess he may have caught it in the bike chain when he jumped off. Once again, Neen came to the rescue.

Then there came the day she saved my life, but that's a story for another time.

As you can imagine, Janine Hawkes was a well-loved figure around Yaraka. Apart from being a first-rate nurse, she was a good friend to many, and a valuable contributor to community life in this very small outback town.

John Paul Tully, retired grazier, Queensland

Hungry the Horse

KIMBERLEY REGION, WESTERN AUSTRALIA

When you work in a remote community you end up being much more than just a nurse. This was certainly the case for me and my partner, when one day a newborn foal of a wild horse was brought into our clinic in the remote community of Oombulgurri. The foal had been left by its mother and could not stand or walk, so a couple of dingos were in the process of eating her. They had started on her rump.

We did not have high hopes for her as she could not even lift her head; she was dehydrated and in shock. But we did what we could and with out-of-date stock that we kept for animal emergencies we placed an intravenous cannula and started to rehydrate her. We also commenced antibiotics to prevent the dingo bites from becoming infected. Soon enough she perked up and we were able to start feeding her powdered milk, at first syringing the milk into her mouth until she was able to lift her head to drink out of the container.

During this first day we gave her regular pressure area care, turning her every couple of hours. By the end of the day we decided that she needed to be put into a standing position just for a minute. We carried her from the clinic to our nice grassy yard to give her something soft to fall on. Carefully we positioned her and supported her into a standing position with both of us holding her. She was very weak and unsteady; if either of us had let her go she would have toppled over. But foals are different from human babies and despite being totally unsteady, she stretched out a foot to take a step. We supported her to take a couple of steps and assisted her back to the ground.

We stayed up late that night to make sure she was okay and to give her the last antibiotic for the day. With such a sick animal, it was in the back of our minds that she may not make it through the night. We woke early to check on her; she was alive and she was hungry! She could suck down a container of milk quicker than a Yankauer sucker could. We continued her care as we had done the day before. We also attempted to keep her cool by placing her in the shade and wiping her down throughout the day. The days were on average 43 degrees and she appeared to be running extra hot due to the dingo bites, which were red, swollen and painful. After work we stood her up again; she was still unsteady and we thought she would have fallen if either of us had stopped supporting her, but she was having none of this. She took a few unsteady steps then started to run. She could run in a straight line okay, but turning and stopping were a problem. You could see the happiness in her face as ran and she gained confidence.

There was no stopping her now; she was mobile and she was hungry!

It didn't take long to fall in love with Hungry. She was loving and cheeky, but she was not the best-looking horse we had ever seen; she had a wall-eye and a lumpy rump.

All horse owners would agree that horses are expensive to keep. Hungry was no exception. She would go through a large bag of 'calf' powdered milk a week. We had to get this flown into the community as this was the only way to get stores in. Luckily for us the local airways were very helpful and would bring them out for free if they had a plane coming out.

Hungry grew and grew and remained hungry, but she was not interested in eating grass like a regular horse, she only wanted milk and she had no problem letting us know!

After nine months of caring for Hungry we started looking for a suitable home for her. After many phone calls, we found a horse trainer who trained with love and not force. He also trained Indigenous children to care for horses and to ride. This seemed like a perfect fit for Hungry.

The next hurdle was to get Hungry to him. She couldn't fly; the only option was to put her on a barge. It was the saddest day to see Hungry go, and to add to this she was scared and stressed. But the horse trainer was true to his word and stayed in the horse float with her the entire twenty-four-hour barge trip.

Hungry got to grow up in a happy, carefree environment with other horses. She was weaned off the milk and her name was changed to 'Oombi' to reflect where she came from. She was trained with love and is now a working horse near Alice Springs; she apparently loves to work and is miffed if she doesn't get to go out.

So if you ever see a big, beautiful horse with a wall-eye, a lumpy rump and a cheeky personality, you are probably looking at Hungry. Say hi from me.

Shelley Munro, rural remote nurse practitioner, lecturer Charles Sturt University

Scaly Surprise

DERBY, WESTERN AUSTRALIA

I am a midwife and I work in a remote maternity unit. One day I had to go out in the ambulance to collect a pregnant lady who was apparently in labour. Unfortunately this woman was a heavy drinker and subsequently, a frequent caller of the ambulance. As per usual this woman was brought back to the maternity unit for assessment and sobering up.

While she was sitting up in the labour ward bed with the CTG (cardio-topography) monitor attached, she proceeded to tell me about the snake in her bag. It was about handover time, so the night duty midwife was also listening to the story. I said to the woman that I didn't believe her, but in her drunken stupor she proceeded to assure us that there was indeed a snake in her bag. I asked her to show me and she agreed.

At this point my colleague quickly departed the room, saying that she was terrified of snakes. I lifted the woman's bag, which was curiously rather heavy, onto the labour bed. I took a few steps back as she started to rummage around in her bag and mumble that she was intending to eat the snake for dinner.

To my shock and amusement the woman finally hauled out a massive black-headed python and dumped it on the bed between her legs. As I called my colleague back to see the sight before me, which you would only see in a remote setting, the patient and I both started to laugh.

My colleague returned but only made it as far as the labour ward door before screaming loudly and running away. Regretfully, I found my colleague very distressed in the nurse's station, stating that she would not be able to take over from me until the snake was removed from the building.

Being pretty keen to go home myself, I went back into the labour ward and asked the woman to put her snake away. I then proceeded to put her bag outside, lock the door and shut the curtains. Despite all of this commotion the CTG continued to run smoothly even though it was a very flat 'drunk' trace.

I am pleased to say that my colleague has forgiven me and now when someone says they are scared of something I believe them.

By the way, the snake was dead.

Vanessa Page, registered nurse

A Snake is a Snake

AMPILATWATJA, NORTHERN TERRITORY

We've been doing this for about six years. We come from the Blue Mountains and Sydney. We were going to a Third World place, probably Africa, when the opportunity came up for us to go up and relieve for a couple of weeks at Ampilatwatja, near Utopia, north-east of Alice Springs.

It was such a great experience we joined an agency and went to Balgo in Western Australia for two years. I was the clinical coordinator for the Kutjunka area while Rhonda worked as RAN at the clinic.

I was walking along one day and Vikki was following me. I saw this thing on the ground and thought, *That's not a stick*, and started walking backwards but when I ran into Vikki she started pushing me forward saying, 'C'mon. Let's go!' I'm saying, 'No, no,' knowing I can't tell her it's a snake because she terrified of them. Finally she's pushing so hard I say, 'It's a snake!' By the time I turned around she was gone!

She'd taken off, but she'd actually gone and found a local boy who thought he might have scored an easy lunch. When they got back, he took one look and said, 'No, I don't want that. It's a poisonous snake. It might bite me. I don't want that.' At the same time, I'm saying, 'We just want to get rid of it . . .' He was no help! He wandered off and the snake wriggled under our house. We went into the house and turned the airconditioner on freezing in the hope it would be too cold for it to come inside.

I got kind of used to snakes eventually. A couple of years later, we were working up at Borroloola. One day, we'd changed a tyre on our 4WD and we'd just finished when we decided we should give it a good clean; we hadn't done it for months. Rhonda walked round to the back of the car and there was a king brown, right there! We let that one go, but I was a bit stunned to see it since we'd been kneeling on the ground changing the tyre a few minutes before.

Next day, we'd just come home for lunch break and Rhonda sat down on the lounge. I went over to the kitchen to wash up a couple of things in the sink. I lifted up the tea towel and there was a small snake lying under it. I stepped back and yelped, 'Snake, snake!'

Rhonda watched the snake slither all over the bench while I rang Edna, an elderly white lady who works at the clinic, to get someone to help. She couldn't find anyone else so she came herself. She said, 'Have you got tongs, a hammer and a sharp knife?'

I'm like, 'Right, okay, yeees.' The tongs weren't very strong but Edna's got a hold of the head with the tongs while I hit it with the hammer. I said, 'What do you want me to do with the knife?' She said, 'Cut its head off.' So I'm there sawing away with knife. Off came the head. She picked it all up, took it outside and said, 'Okay, see you back at the clinic.'

We think it was a death adder. We've got a photo of it.

Rhonda Smith and Vikki Robertson, registered nurses

chapter seven

SOME DAYS ARE DIAMOND

In amongst the often monotonous, sometimes challenging, occasionally tragic days experienced by rural and remote nurses, there are cameo days when something funny, extraordinary and/or just plain warm and fuzzy makes all the other days totally worthwhile.

The Apprentice

NORTH-WEST NEW SOUTH WALES

Hospital trained, I returned to my local community without any post-graduating experience. It was literally a matter of sink or swim – fast! I was taught to suture on only my second late shift, by the wardsmaid! A couple of blokes had belted each other over the head and required their matching scalp lacerations to be stitched up. I thought it was time to recall the matron until persuaded otherwise by my colleague. I phoned the Royal Flying Doctor Service (RFDS) who reinforced that it would be *me* performing this exercise on not one, but two victims; I considered them victims, not of each other, but of this *very* junior 'sister'! *Okay*, I thought, *so I* have *seen it done before*, but I muttered, 'How in the hell am I going to do this by myself?'

'No worries!' I was assured by the said wardsmaid. She retrieved a block of chipboard from the cupboard beneath the outpatient's sink. A foam pad covered in red vinyl sat atop this rather tired masterpiece, with a split down the length of it. After a demonstration it was my turn to bring these edges together, the closest one could get to 'doing the real thing', I was told. After all, the texture did mimic that of human tissue – sort of. First push the needle through the tough dermis, into soft tissue and out the other tough side with a bit of a tug.

Tying knots was the easy part!

Victim one kindly lay down on the trolley and went to sleep, oblivious to the novice operating on him. Job done! Victim two was not so cooperative. He insisted on sitting upright, having the hide to question why my hands were shaking. I gave them both the 'return if any concerns, sutures out in seven days' lecture. I never did see either of them again so perhaps that meant the sutures fell out themselves. I just hoped there was good wound union and that they at least lasted a few days!

Jane Clarke, registered nurse

Morning Smoko with Jacko

OODNADATTA, NORTHERN SOUTH AUSTRALIA

As part of our patient care program we visited a few of our elderly Indigenous folk at home who would otherwise miss out on vital medication. One of my favourites was Jacko, who lived with his wife and extended family in one of the numerous camps that dotted the town. Jacko was a proud old fella who led a quiet life in his camp and made horse hobbles and carved native animals from gigi tree branches. He was a family elder and well respected by everyone, but no longer played an active part in tribal gatherings as he had a failing heart.

As far as we could ascertain he was between seventy-five

and eighty years old considering that he'd been a soldier in
World War I as a young fella and re-joined the army during
WW II. After returning home he'd worked on the land for
many years as a drover, before eventually settling in town
about a decade ago when his poor health forced him to lead
a sedentary life. As his children drifted away from town, his
source of more traditional tucker dried up and his pension
money was spent buying basic perishables from the store. His
years on the land had his tastebuds still yearning for goanna,
lizard and kangaroo, which had become a treat and not the
norm in his diet.

One particular morning as I drove up to Jacko's place I
was alarmed at the amount of smoke billowing from his backyard fire and quickly entered his gate thinking that I'd have to
extinguish a blaze. With my nose twitching and eyes water-
ing at the dreadful smell of burning fur emanating from the
camp fire, I was taken aback at seeing a big grey kangaroo car-
cass draped over the shallow fire pit with flames licking up its
flanks. The large roo's body was still fully furred and its open
abdomen spilt pink entrails from a chest-to-tail cut. Its limp,
long tail extended well beyond the glowing coals and would
be savoured as a tasty titbit later in the day. I was forced to
control my roiling stomach as Jacko proudly showed me his
delicacy and invited me back for some tucker 'when him big
fella cooked'. Needless to say, I declined his generous offer and
suggested that he save some for the family.

Most days Jacko popped over to the community nurse's
place for morning smoko, where he enjoyed sweet black tea
and biscuits. When the community nurse was away he'd invite
the hospital nurse to join him for smoko when we dropped in

his tablets. Being prepared for his invitation to join him for smoko, we'd pack a few bickies into a container and bring our own mug. Perched on a log in my white uniform, I'd listen to the most amazing stories of his youth and time spent on the land in bygone days, and watch his rheumy eyes mist over as he lamented their passing.

One of his biggest concerns was for those in his community who'd succumbed to the temptation of the bottle, and Jacko felt saddened that many members of his community had lost their tribal ways and become dependent on 'white fellas' for their survival.

In keeping with our traditional landowners' beliefs, I have called this proud Australian Jacko so that his spirit may continue to rest in Dreamtime and not be disturbed by mentioning his real name.

Sue Nilon, retired registered nurse

Sharing Women's Business

CENTRAL NORTHERN TERRITORY

This is a lovely story about the experiences I have had with Aboriginal people working out in a remote community. I live in Brisbane and work as an RAN (remote area nurse) doing relief work through an agency for up to six months at a time.

In one community, I was able to go out with the women

looking for bush food, bush medicines and raw materials for their crafts. I was lucky enough to have that opportunity and go to some wonderful and amazing places and experience all the different age groups together, with older women passing their knowledge on to younger women. I learnt a lot about the bush and learnt how to prepare some of their bush medicines, where to find them and how to use them.

I used to try and organise trips out with the women every other week, depending on how many 4WDs were available. One week my husband was coming up to stay and it was the week that we normally did an outing. Because it was women's business I thought we wouldn't be able to do the trip because it's something the women do. I talked to one of the elders about it. She put her hands on her hips and declared very assertively, 'They need to know as well!' She was quite forceful about it.

There were other people in town that week so we ended up having seven 4WDs to go out on the trip. There were all different age groups, from grandmothers down to babies. I had a couple of older women in the troopy with me and the elder, who was in her late seventies, was in another vehicle. She stopped along the track, but the women in my car said they wouldn't get out because there was nothing there. They said the elder's eyesight wasn't good any more and she couldn't see. It was lovely watching the way they interacted and worked things out. We eventually moved on to another place that everyone was happy to go to.

We got out and we started digging for honey ants. The women were using digging sticks they'd brought with them, but I had a spade I'd brought. I was digging away and the elder pushed me aside, saying I was no good at it, so my husband had a go because she said he had the muscles. After a while, she pushed him away too, saying, 'None of you are very good. I'll have to show you all how to do it.' And so she did and it is a real art. It was interesting watching her and the other women and how they worked together.

On these trips to their country I always used to buy kangaroo tails to take with us to cook up while we were there. It was interesting to see how they served up, deciding who got what. There was my husband with the most beautiful piece of kangaroo tail presented so beautifully to him on a bark plate and I was thinking, *That's a bit unfair*, but that's just the way it is.

We had some other young men, white fellas, who were there that day that were visiting the community as well, and the women were really keen to share their knowledge with all of them. They took the time to take us around and show us their country. It was a real privilege.

I try to go back to the same communities because there is continuity then. I know the people when I go back. I've done many different things, often on my own or sometimes with other nurses. I have learnt that you can take the good ideas that work in one community and share the information with other communities. However, it is up to that community whether they decide to use the ideas.

Many people I've met have tended to live in the moment. For instance, one day we were all busy collecting bush medicines for the women to take to a women's meeting they were going to. We spent hours going out collecting the raw material and coming back and preparing everything. You notice a wonderful sense of sharing as they're going about their business.

The knowledge is handed down through the generations. The women talk amongst themselves as they're working and deciding what to do. While you're out there, they tell their stories, talking about the country and what's needed and what's available at any given time. It's very, very special to be included.

On this particular occasion, it got too hot so I said, 'Let's leave it and we'll get it all together in the morning and then it'll be ready to take.' At times, everything is done at the last minute. So next morning, we got it all together and they were so excited but then someone came along and said something else needed doing, and so the bush medicine was just left. They took off to do whatever the next important thing was and forgot about the medicines. I just gave the bundles to one of the drivers to give to them when they got there.

Kathy Wooldridge registered nurse, BN, MACN

Bush Medicine

KIMBERLEY REGION, WESTERN AUSTRALIA

An elderly Aboriginal man came in to the hospital to have his prostate gland removed. He arrived resplendent in his new gear and an enormous 10-gallon hat. It could only be removed when he was anaesthetised! He was a small man and was quite a sight sitting up in bed under his huge hat.

After his surgery, he became disorientated and started to remove all his dressings. Consequently, his wound became infected. No amount of antibiotics had any effect on the infection. He got agitated and kept muttering in his own language about his wound.

An Aboriginal orderly who could speak English said that the man wanted some ant bed. So, in the hospital Land Rover, we went to knock down some ant bed. We took it back to the old man and his face lit up. He took the ant bed, ground it up, spat on it until he made a paste and then applied it to his wound. He allowed me to put a dressing on it but then I had to leave it for ten days.

When the dressing was removed, the wound was healed. We were amazed. A sample of the ant bed dust was sent to Perth for analysis. It was found to be a form of streptomycin.

Adapted from a story by Nan Farmer, Derby District Hospital, 1963–1970, courtesy of the Kimberley Nurses History Group publication, Boughsheds, Boabs and Bandages: Stories of Nursing in the Kimberley

My Darling Darling
KIMBERLEY REGION, WESTERN AUSTRALIA

There are particular moments and particular people who stay with you long after you have left a job and an area. I was nursing in a remote town on an eight-week contract. It was a 'fill in time' and 'fill up the bank balance' job before I made more permanent plans.

An elderly Indigenous man had been admitted for some respite and care. He was dying from cancer and his wife usually provided all care for him. However, they lived on a remote community and it became difficult at times to sustain the level of care he needed. This elderly couple had a special something between them and the devotion of the wife to her husband was truly beautiful.

She would assist the nursing staff as much as possible with all his cares and was always ready at his side should he need her. There were many moments of giggles. For instance, when we would try to roll him over to do his cares and he would accidentally grab his wife's bosom, or when I showed her the device I would use to roll over her husband's penis to fit him with a urine bag. She thought this was absolutely hilarious and said that the device was *much* too small.

This man was a fully initiated Aboriginal man who spoke limited English. I think he understood everything but chose not to speak to us much; his eyes did most of the communicating. One morning we were attending to this man's morning shower and after washing him and dressing him in the bathroom, I pushed him out in his wheelchair to where his wife was waiting. I said, 'Look, there is your lovely wife.' And in a very gruff voice he said, 'That's not my lovely wife.' I was a bit shocked, but in the next breath he stated, 'That is my darling Darling.'

I was so moved by this couple and their love.

Aggie Harpham, registered nurse

Laughter's the Best Medicine

KIMBERLEY REGION, WESTERN AUSTRALIA

I was a local impressionable fifteen-year-old assistant nurse (there were no registered nursing aides at that time) and was excited, fascinated and eager, so I soaked up everything there was to learn.

The hospital was old and sort of condemned by the health law because every now and then the kitchen chimney plugged up and caught on fire and smoked the place out. We would have to phone the pub for all hands on deck to put out the fire. This happened regularly, about once a month. We also had a big bell stand that we had to run out and ring.

Other than the Flying Doctor, at Derby Hospital there were twenty-eight beds and outpatients to deal with in a day's work. We had to do routine urine testing the old way for all admissions, with a few crystals of this or that, and a few drops of this or that and shake it up and boil it over a Bunsen burner, being very careful so it wouldn't shoot all over the place.

Cultures for throat swabs of infections were put in Petri dishes that then went into the incubator. There was no lab until 1958, I think.

The new Flying Doctor base was opened in 1959 and the governor-general and Lady Gairdner were present to officiate. Then they were to come over to the hospital to visit. We were meant to be all starched and looking our best; however, an Aboriginal woman came in to have her twelfth baby and interrupted the whole show. Lady Gairdner visited the patients and when she asked the woman how she felt, she said, 'Just like taking a big shit, missus!'

Though we worked hard, there was always something that happened during our busy day to give you a laugh. One day, during outpatients, a jackaroo came up to see the doctor.

'Can I help you?' I asked.

'Yes,' he said. 'I've got the clap.'

I told the doctor, so when he went in, the doctor said, 'You shouldn't be so crude to the nurse. If she asks what's wrong, tell her you have something wrong with your ear.'

So when the guy got to outpatients and I asked what I could do to help him, he said, 'I can't pee out of my ear.'

Adapted extract from 'Derby District Hospital' by Faye Smith (Laackman) 1955–1962 Courtesy of the Kimberley Nurses History Group publication, Boughsheds, Boabs and Bandages: Stories of Nursing in the Kimberley

Cops and Robbers
NORTH-WEST NEW SOUTH WALES

It was my first ambulance call-out in a small community. The call came through that a man was having an asthma attack on the steps of the post office, and he's 'in a real bad way, sister'. This fellow was known to other staff.

I was given a brief history on his background, and it was stated that he 'mustn't be too good' to actually request assistance; a bit of a 'tough' character, I was informed. *Great,* I thought, *first ever time on ambulance call and I end up with a real emergency!*

Off we go, planning already underway for respiratory support. I thought we may even need to prepare for aminophylline infusion so had everything ready to go. I hadn't successfully cannulated before, so the main plan was to get him back to the hospital asap.

On arriving at the post office, I found a large man sitting on the steps with moderate respiratory distress. *All good,* I thought. I determined I had enough time to get him back to the hospital to commence any infusions. I jumped out of the ambulance and on approaching this fellow I had more than a few obscenities thrown at me for 'taking my time'. He yelled at me, 'Gimme a f***ing puffer!' I had wondered why the girls had given me one as I left the hospital, when I was preparing for something much bigger.

As he lumbered towards me, I retreated and threw the damn thing at him! He puffed away on it then ran off! *That wasn't supposed to happen,* I thought. *What the hell am I going to tell Matron?* I was called out and didn't have any show and tell to take back with me. How did I explain that I didn't have a patient and, even worse, how could I complete my assessment and paperwork?

As I stood there pondering how to explain myself to Matron, the police came tearing around the corner. They stopped and asked if I had a seen a man fitting a particular description.

'I sure have!' I proudly told them. 'He was my first ambulance call-out!'

They thanked me *very* much for giving him some fresh wind to allow him to take off again. They had been trying to catch him for several hours!

Jane Clarke, registered nurse

Appreciation

HIGH COUNTRY, VICTORIA

Early one morning I was called to a little boy about nine or ten years of age. He had got up very early and had been on his way after the cows, when he could not go any further. He lay on the grass wet with dew and slept until found there, still fast asleep. When they tried to wake him to go on after the cows, they realised he was ill so sent for me.

I found him gravely ill and decided to take him straight to Dr Ley, 25 miles (40 kilometres) from my cottage. I had to nurse the boy all the way, as he just could not be made comfortable any other way and it seemed the most awkward position I moved to was the most comfortable for him.

I would get stiff and try to get a little more comfortable but, as sure as I did so, he would moan and be restless. So there was nothing else to do but just stay uncomfortable and get very stiff.

When Dr Ley saw the boy, he marvelled that I carried him

all that way. At once he called Mrs Ley and said: 'This is our wonderful bush nurse. I would be pleased, dear, if you would take her with you to the hall and look after her. She is very tired but a change will do her good.'

I tried to get out of going, but could not do so without being absolutely rude. I was so tired and would have liked a good rest and sleep. But, away we went and I overheard doctor say to Mrs Ley, 'Give her a good time. Tell the doctors to lionise her.' They were all wonderful to me but I was honestly very glad when I was on my way home again. The boy had rheumatic fever.

Extracts adapted from Memoirs of a Victorian Bush Nurse in the 1920s *by Alice Martin, registered nurse and midwife, transcribed by her daughter, Val Watson*

chapter eight

ON DEATH AND DYING

---

*The one sure thing about life is death. Sharing
the journey is an experience nurses generally consider
a privilege.*

A Special Brand of Bush Care

CENTRAL NORTHERN TERRITORY

On 28 January 2004, at the age of fifty-four, my husband Allen was diagnosed with motor neurone disease (MND). We were living in Willowra, a remote Indigenous community three and a half hours from Alice Springs, out in the Tanami Desert. I was the community nurse and Allen was our part-time clinic gardener, cleaner and driver. He was also employed part-time in the community school where, in a somewhat bizarre twist, he was working with a young disabled lad in a wheelchair, striving to improve the boy's independence.

A remote community probably sounds like the worst possible place to be, in the circumstances, but it proved to be quite the opposite.

After Allen's diagnosis, we made the joint decision to stay in Willowra. Allen's attitude to his illness was that he had 'ten good years ahead so let's get on with enjoying life'. We were already booked to fly to Cambodia for our annual leave, a journey we had been making each year since year 2000, to do voluntary work in an orphanage. Before we'd moved to Willowra, Allen had spent his spare time collecting unwanted pushbikes and refurbishing them. He would then fill a shipping container with the bikes and other goods and dispatch them to Cambodia prior to our yearly departure.

In 2003, we'd taken our son Aaron with us to help Allen pour concrete floors in buildings we were refurbishing at the orphanage and he had returned to Cambodia to teach English. Our forthcoming visit this time was extra special because Aaron was marrying his Khmer fiancée.

We flew out as planned in April, ten weeks after Allen's diagnosis. On the day of the wedding Allen had his first fall; he blamed the grass for catching his foot. We flew from Cambodia to Laos to continue our holiday and it was noticeable that Allen was tiring easily; he was, until now, a man who had always had boundless energy. After fourteen days in Laos we flew back to Cambodia and into Siem Reap, where we celebrated our thirty-third wedding anniversary at the outdoor market with a two-course meal and a Klang beer for the princely sum of $2.50. 'Pity we won't make it to our fiftieth anniversary,' Allen remarked. This was the first indication that he had accepted his life was going to be cut short.

While on holiday we realised his legs were weakening, and we decided to ask my boss for a transfer to a community on the bitumen . . . still remote, but without the danger of closed roads in the rain. We returned to Willowra after a wonderful six-week holiday, and I packed the house with very mixed emotions. We moved to Ti Tree, about 200 kilometres north of Alice Springs on the Stuart Highway, where our house was 100 metres from the clinic.

Soon after this Allen began walking with the aid of wrist crutches. Our DMO (district medical officer) suggested to me that we have a visit from the palliative care team from Alice Springs. I was absolutely horrified. My initial response was,

'No way!' In my mind palliative care meant dying and I was not ready to face that prospect.

However, after my initial negative reaction our DMO talked to me about making early contact with appropriate agencies and services as a long-term strategy, whether or not we would need them in the short term. And so the amazing Fred Miegel, palliative care nurse, entered our life and what an important part of it he was to become for both of us.

Fred's compassionate honesty at our first meeting prepared me mentally and emotionally for the journey ahead. Twelve years previously we had watched Allen's father, at the age of sixty-eight, succumb to the same illness over a two-and-a-half-year period. We knew the journey ahead.

Allen was adamant that he wasn't going to get to the same stage as his father. He was afraid of being 'kept alive' in a totally helpless state, unable to communicate with his loved ones. He had always been so active and he could think of nothing worse. Fred talked to us both about the role of palliative care, and Allen's rights and options in refusing life-prolonging care. He explained the Natural Death Act. We talked about a lot of things, most of which I don't remember, *but* I have a very clear recollection of us both feeling empowered and at ease at the end of the two-and-a-half-hour session.

In time, Fred introduced us to the other members of the palliative care team, who travelled up from Alice Springs to see us regularly. No words can adequately describe that team and their support. The remote physiotherapist and occupational therapist (OT) came on board and, as Allen's needs changed over time, the appropriate aids and equipment just appeared with the visiting team members.

Within six months, I was caring for Allen completely and working full-time as an RAN at the clinic. My shoulders ached constantly from lifting. Our DMO contacted the Alice Springs Carer's Respite Association and, through them, a carer was funded to shower Allen alternate days, relieving some of the physical stress on my body. In addition, Carer's Respite funded an hour's massage for me on our monthly visits to Alice Springs – a godsend!

When Allen began experiencing swallowing difficulties, the allied health team brought the speech pathologist with them; another delightful lady. She assessed his problems and provided advice and strategies to assist, though she was never able to convince him that a beer would taste the same with thickener in it!

By October, nine months from diagnosis, Allen had gone from riding his pushbike daily to crutches, to walking frame, to wheelchair. At each stage the transition was handled with empathy and dignity by the various team members. When the physio initially brought the walking frame after several falls, he stubbornly refused to use it. She respected his wishes, and took it away without argument; by her next visit, much to my relief, he had come to his own decision that he needed it.

I was stunned at the relentless rapidity of Allen's deterioration. His positive, determined outlook and the medication had not slowed the symptoms at all. I knew the average prognosis in Australia was twenty-nine months from diagnosis and it was apparent that Al was going to spend most of that time in a wheelchair. He was absolutely determined to make our annual trip to Cambodia the following March/April, both to visit our son and his wife and the kids at the orphanage who, after five years, had become such an important part of our lives. My fear was that we would struggle to keep him hydrated in the heat and humidity, as drinking was becoming a slower process.

I raised the subject of a PEG tube. He found the mere thought abhorrent and flatly refused to discuss the idea. Even Fred and the DMO were unable to convince him of the merits of a tube for fluids. I didn't want to pressure him, but I also wanted to know he would be safe on holidays. The very next issue of the MND support group newsletter featured articles and photos from members who had had PEG surgery, all speaking positively about the benefits.

After digesting the articles, Al began asking questions and agreed to the procedure on the express understanding that he was in control and when he refused fluids, his wishes would be respected. About this time he also decided it was time to sign the papers for the Natural Death Act in the NT and the corresponding papers for South Australia. This was done at home in Ti Tree with our DMO, Fred and the local police officer as witness.

In late November, twenty-four hours before he was due for admission to Alice Springs hospital for the surgery, Allen was hit with a sudden viral upper respiratory tract infection. His admission went ahead after our DMO conferred with the surgical registrar, the plan being to commence antibiotics while surgery was postponed for a day or so. Then, disaster! The night before his scheduled surgery Allen suffered a sudden aspiration. Surgery was again delayed and we found ourselves in a catch-22. Anaesthesia now posed a very real risk, but equally risky was delaying surgery, as oral fluids were now an added danger.

Allen now looked dreadfully ill, and for the first time in his illness I felt very afraid. Suddenly we were no longer preparing for Cambodia in March; we just wanted to get to Christmas.

Surgery was rescheduled, and recovery was slow. Allen was deteriorating rapidly. He was in pain, tired and nauseated. I had a divan in his hospital room so I could be with him for twenty-four-hour assistance. Fred and the pal care team visited us daily, often twice a day; their emotional support was incredible. After nearly a month in hospital we finally flew to Adelaide for Christmas with all the family. Allen had the joy of holding his first grandchild all the way from Cambodia.

On Boxing Day he was more concerned with the tsunami victims than his own health and needs, and then on New Year's Day we flew back to Alice Springs with our daughter-in-law and grandson, and drove to Ti Tree. I gave a month's notice at work. On 30 January – my fifty-fifth birthday – exactly one year on from diagnosis, we moved to our newly completed cottage on the Yorke Peninsula in South Australia. Fred and our wonderful pal care team from Alice Springs had made contact with community health on Southern Yorke Peninsula, and everything we needed was waiting for us. The new team stepped in for a seamless transition.

Allen passed away at home ten weeks later surrounded by his family.

About two and a half years later, lying in bed one night, I suddenly realised how fortunate we had been to be where we were at the time of diagnosis. In the bush the terrain is flat and the buildings are all single so no stairs. There was no driving for doctor's appointments and no parking worries.

If we had still been living in Adelaide, we would have been in our upstairs apartment with stairs. I could not have continued working; I would have been afraid to leave Allen at home and we would never have been able to build our beach cottage, Allen's lifelong dream. In fact it is impossible for me to imagine what life would have been like.

For twelve months we had a multidisciplinary allied health team involved in our lives. The various members worked cohesively, communicating closely with us and each other. They felt more like friends than health team members. Allen and I were involved in all decision making with them and we always felt in command of our life.

Friends often asked how we were managing in the bush, and our answer was that we received better and more personal care than we would have in the city. We had support in the physical sense, but, just as importantly, we had emotional support. We received truly holistic care, and could not have wished for more.

Sue Leverton, registered nurse (remote)

Postscript: Sue asked that this story be dedicated to Allen and their children, as well as the wonderful people in Central Australia Remote Health and Southern Yorke Peninsula Community Health, South Australia.

Consideration

KIMBERLEY REGION, WESTERN AUSTRALIA

During corroboree time on the station, the old house gardener came up from the camp to tell me that one old man from Nicholson was 'a bit short of wind'. I asked that he be brought up to the big house, but the gardener asked me to go to the camp. When I arrived, I looked at the old man and said to the gardener, 'I think he has run out of wind,' to which he answered, 'Youeye' (you right). When I inquired why he hadn't told me the old man had died, he replied, 'I didn't want to frighten you, missus.'

Helen Macarthur, Gordon Downs Station

Adapted extract from 'Helen Macarthur, Gordon Downs Station', courtesy of the Kimberley Nurses History Group publication Boughsheds, Boabs and Bandages: Stories of Nursing in the Kimberley

Destiny

NORTH QUEENSLAND

The lady came into the emergency department. Cancer had ravaged her body for two years and she was very sick. She told me that if I took her naso-gastric tube out, it would never go in again. I felt a strong connection with this lady. I do that with people; make connections. It helps me to win the trust of my patients and do my job better. When I read her chart and saw her address, I knew somehow, one day, I would visit this place. She was being admitted and that was the end of it.

Shortly after, I was called in for a night shift on medical ward and during handover I was surprised to hear this lady was still a patient. She was not my patient but I felt compelled to talk to her, to somehow reach out. I read her chart during the night and in the morning, I made an excuse to go in her room and talk to her. She didn't remember me and wasn't particularly friendly. I said goodbye and went home.

A few weeks later, my sister rang me. She is also a nurse and had heard on the grapevine about a job out on an isolated cattle property. We both wanted to do remote nursing but had families to think about and had never been in a situation to have a go. She said that there was a job looking after a lady who was dying and wanted to stay at home. I knew instinctively that it was my lady. I said to her, 'I already know this lady,' and she asked, 'How could you?' I told her that I just knew that I had a destiny with this person and started to tell her the story. She told me that I was wrong because the lady was much older than mine. I interrupted her because I was so certain and I told her the name of the property. She was astounded and asked me how I knew, but I had no answer. She said, 'You are going to take this job, aren't you.'

I rang the lady from the Frontier Services program who was handling the process of looking for a nurse and inquired about the job. I was told that she had a large and supportive network of family and friends already there but they needed a carer on hand to support them. I told them that I would think about it.

At the time, I was an endorsed enrolled nurse and had always been able to pass the buck to the senior nurse when the going got tough. As I reflected on the implications of this unique opportunity, I wondered if I could cope emotionally with this life and death on my own, way out there on an isolated property with no senior nurse to back me up. I would have to leave my husband and children, who are my rocks. Would I be able to be the nurse that this family needed me to be? Suddenly, I thought about my sisters and I prayed that someone would be there if this was one of them, so I agreed to do it.

Frontier Services told me I would be employed as a carer, not a nurse, and asked me how much I wanted to be paid; I felt compelled to tell them I would accept whatever they were offering. My husband gently chastised me for that but I felt driven to do this. As always, he respected my wishes and trusted that I would make the right decision. So it was settled; I would be going in a few days.

Now my mind went into overdrive: *What if she had a big bleed? Take a reality check! You are going to help her to die, not save her life!* Within days I would be off to the unknown. I notified my boss at the local hospital where I was employed casually that I would be unavailable for an unknown amount of time. I had a session with the doctor who would be my only contact with the medical world via two-way radio. She assured me that I would be fine, hadn't I been a nurse for nearly thirty years? Of course I would be fine, I kept telling myself.

The lady from Frontier Services, who was taking me part

of the way, asked me if I would have a problem doing the last part of the journey on a helicopter. I love flying and immediately visualised a helicopter in the movies with all the army guys bravely jumping out of it. This sounded very exciting and I enthusiastically declared, 'I would love it!'

The big day came and off we went. After driving for a few hours we arrived at an airport where we were met with what I thought was a motorbike with a glass bubble on it. *Oh no, this was it? Where was my big exciting helicopter?* I was going for a ride in a mustering chopper; it didn't even have doors! *Be cool, be brave, you can do this, just act nonchalant. What were they saying? I couldn't take my belongings, there wasn't room! Great!*

They asked if I would mind carrying flowers on my lap for my lady. 'No worries,' I said. Lucky I love flowers! So there I was, sitting in a little bubble with a great big bunch of flowers between my legs and about to trust some stranger with my life. The 'stranger' jumped in beside me. *Oh no, this couldn't be happening, the pilot looks about sixteen.* He informed me that he was my pilot and I'd better be prepared as there was a storm ahead. *Bloody wonderful.*

I jokingly asked him, 'You do have a licence to fly this thing, don't you?' He readily admitted that he did; that it was easy to get one in just six weeks and no, he wasn't only sixteen, he was eighteen! Great stuff! I was saying my prayers that I wouldn't break the seat by holding on so hard. My legs were tightly clamped together; at least the flowers weren't going anywhere.

As we ascended above the cows and trees, my pilot keenly offered to take me for a detour over a mine site for a look. Obviously this young man was completely oblivious to my anxiety levels! I suggested that we bypass this excursion and leave it for another day when it was fine.

On arrival at the station, we were met by a group of family members who were keen to get me settled in. My pilot generously returned later with my luggage. I was already homesick and I hadn't even seen my patient yet.

The family's patriarch and his wife and family lived in one house and my lady lived across the paddock in the old house. I was to stay with her and her friend who had come from down south to spend her last days with her. It was extremely hot; the house was old but fine. The only water was in a tank and needed to be carried in in buckets and there were lots of bugs and creepy crawlies. *What was I thinking?* I wondered. I decided I was going to make the best of this and nothing was going to stand in my way.

I quickly assessed the patient and realised that she had deteriorated dramatically since our last encounter a month before. There was no weight left on her and she was not able to keep anything down. I had been told that she did not want to take morphine; I had weighed up the options with the consulting doctor before leaving. I had it with me but would not use it unless absolutely necessary. It had been made quite clear to the patient and family that if she chose to have intravenous fluids, she would have to go into hospital. There would be no lifesaving mercy flights; she was going to die.

She was such a strong character who had lived life to the full and was not going to go easily. She was an only girl who worked alongside her brothers on the property. Her friend was amazing and I hoped that my friendships were this strong. She would do whatever my lady asked of her, which included diary keeping. My lady kept a diary on a daily basis, which her friend kept right up to hours before her death. How strong was this woman who felt it was so important to still be in control right up to the very end? She noticed any single thing out of place, right down to weeds outside in the house yard.

I had brought my aromatherapy oils and decided that massage would be the most therapeutic approach. So began the first of my twelve days out there.

Day two commenced with the power going down and it would stay out for two days, which meant no fans, etc. It also meant no two-way radio, my only connection to the real world. Wow! Now I really was in culture shock.

I set up a stretcher beside my lady so that she could just tap me if she needed me. We spent our days massaging from head to toe, in silence most of the time. She started dreaming about swimming in the river though she admitted that she had never been fond of swimming. I figured that it was because of her body's need for fluids.

I asked her brothers if there was any way we could give her a soak. Before long, I was called outside and lo and behold a bathtub had appeared. We filled it up with the hose and prepared for the big plunge. One of her brothers carried her down the stairs. This was heaven for her, or close to it, and I thought to myself, *Why didn't I think of this sooner?* It quickly developed into a ritual and each day we would spend time with her laying in the tub spotting the weeds and me removing them.

One day she announced that she felt like some Coca-Cola to drink, though she had apparently never liked it in her life. We didn't have any Coke on the property and were now faced with a challenge to come up with some. Her brother got on the two-way and asked if anyone on the neighbouring property could share a can or two. Within hours, from out of the heavens came a carton of Coke; the chopper guys heard the call and took a trip to town, God bless them. My next challenge was to attempt to make jelly with Coke. That is not easy to do and wasn't very successful but I was prepared to try anything to keep up the pretence that she was still eating.

As the days and nights wore on, she became almost lifeless before my eyes and we seemed to have melded days and nights together. We had a spray pump bottle of water with which we would regularly hydrate her externally. The anti-emetics failed eventually and she could keep nothing down. I was feeling so helpless and ineffective.

I wished I had of known her before she became ill as she was an amazing person; such strength. After ten days, she said to me, 'I can't do this any more.' It was as if she'd always felt she had to be strong and not give in or appear weak. I rang the doctor and told them that I felt cruel not doing something else for her. We discussed morphine and decided to start small doses to ease her burden. I told her that I needed to give her something to take her hypersensitivity away. She had become super-sensitive to even the touch of a mosquito. She didn't ask what it was so I took that as consent and gave her the first dose. She stopped taking all oral fluids and the vomiting finally stopped. I don't think there was anything left.

Her brothers asked me to have a meeting with them to discuss what else we could do to make her more comfortable. It was decided to ask the doctor if we could increase the morphine order, which was a minimum dose. She never asked what I gave her, but I'm sure she knew. That night, she kept drifting in and out until after midnight when I finally crashed beside her. At 0200 hours I awoke to her calling, 'Sandy, Sandy, wake up, we've got a big day ahead so you had better spray me down and you might need it too.' I asked her why. What was the big day about? She just looked at me and said, 'I am going to die today, aren't I?' I told her that her time was near but I couldn't promise anything.

Then she got me to wake her friend. She seemed adamant that she had to get everything in order. The diary came out and was updated. By 0400 hours she started ringing her friends and thanking them for their friendship and support. I was in tears by this stage. By 1000 hours, I told her brother that the end wouldn't be far away. I had rung the doctor and was about to give her another dose of morphine. Her body was showing all the signs of death, I could almost smell it around me, but was strangely calm.

Her life was draining away before our eyes. Her other brothers arrived and they all gathered around her to say their last goodbyes, then left for the big house. So there we were; just her, her friend, her sister-in-law and me. She drifted off while we sat talking to her and holding her hands. A flock of cockatoos flew over, all shrieking loudly, and I'm sure she flew off with them.

I went over to the big house to help make arrangements. While her spirit stayed there, her body had to be taken into town for burial. The family had hired a chopper for this purpose. I went back over and we dressed her in her full station working clothes and waited for her final ride. Once her body was onboard, I climbed in the back seat and looked out over the land. Her brother came and placed a bunch of wildflowers on her and we said our goodbyes. The trip into town was much quicker in the big chopper but strangely I don't remember much about it.

My mother and grandmother were both nurses and I had always wanted to do remote nursing; this experience made me go for it. In 2001, I put in an application and was accepted into a Bachelor of Nursing at the James Cook University campus in Mount Isa. For my grad year I went to Normanton and Mornington Island. On return, I commenced a post-grad Cert in Advanced Surgical Nursing followed by Advanced Physiology.

All these years later, I still am deeply touched by this lady I had cared for and what she taught me about myself and life and death. Every time I hear cockies fly over, I think how honoured I am to have shared her journey.

Sandy Hanson, registered nurse, lecturer

Life's End

KALTUKATJARA (DOCKER RIVER), NORTHERN TERRITORY

Palliative care in a remote Aboriginal community setting is one of the most rewarding areas of nursing. Often, English is the third, fourth or even fifth language of most residents. The non-Aboriginal RAN is in the minority and generally has limited understanding of the rituals associated with life ending.

One of our most senior women had refused dialysis and wanted to 'finish up' (die) in her own country. She had many medical problems, including uncontrolled diabetes and cardiac compromise. She caused the RAN much grief with deterioration in her health and 'non-compliance' with recommended treatment over many years. However, she lived with her husband, she cared for grandchildren, nieces and nephews and fostered one little girl from babyhood. She enjoyed going hunting and collecting traditional bush foods. She was pivotal to many traditional ceremonies and had great authority in the community.

Although 'non-compliant' with medicines and western treatment, she used Aboriginal traditional medicines and saw the traditional healers (*ngangkaris*). She was always willing to talk to the RAN; sometimes this involved a search around the community to locate her, and she could always explain why she hadn't done what we wanted of her. Sometimes she 'forgot', other times she was busy or had lost the medicines or had been away hunting or visiting in other communities. Her life was busy and active despite her worsening health.

As time went by, her diabetes worsened and her kidneys began to fail. She had said several times over her last two years that she did not want to go to town for dialysis – she had seen her sister die in town while on dialysis and she did not want to do the same thing. In her last two months she was bedridden and became more and more bloated with fluid. Her husband continued to care for her, hunting food and cooking it while her foster daughter continued to sleep in the same bed with her. Extended family came from many communities to sit with her and she had both the television and phone within reach.

There was only one RAN caring for a community of approximately 300 people so she did not receive daily visits from health professionals. She had never been particularly fastidious about her personal hygiene, having been born in the bush and lived in wurlies most of her life with minimal access to water. She had a house to live in only in the last five years of her life. The RAN visited once a week to help give her a good wash and make sure she was as comfortable as possible. She was so bloated with fluid it was impossible to turn her; however, if bed sores had developed she did not suffer any pain from them. In her last days she sank into a coma and family came to tell the RAN she was now sleeping. Visits were increased to daily, mostly to reassure the family and to check she was still not in pain. On her last day, the RAN told family that her respiratory pattern indicated that it probably wouldn't be long now. At 6 p.m., a senior community man came to tell the RAN she had passed away.

She had been wrapped in her blankets and family and community members were filing through the house to touch her and express their sorrow. When all had done so, the RAN was asked to take her away, so she was zipped into a body bag and six strong community members helped transport her to the makeshift cool room used as a morgue. Family moved out of the house; it was too sad to remain with all its associated memories of the deceased. Her funeral was some weeks later and attended by many people.

Palliative care revolves around making people comfortable at the end of their life. This woman and many others did not receive daily visits from a nurse for nutritional, hygiene or medication management. Families were the primary care givers for nutrition and hygiene. The RANs provided pain management, using syringe drivers supplied by the palliative care unit or inserting a butterfly needle and giving subcutaneous morphine as often as they thought necessary.

Families were reassured by the interest the RANs took in them and their dying relative, as much as by the health care provided. Dying family members remained in their own bedding, surrounded by the sounds and activities they had experienced all their lives and knowing they were still part of the family unit. Families saw and had control over what happened to their relative and were able to move through rituals of grieving without the barriers of western medical care.

Lyn Byers, midwife, nurse practitioner (remote)

The Funeral
NORTHERN TERRITORY

A chilling wail rang out through the community, awakening sleepers. It rose from a cavern of human grief and drowned the western music of the last grog revellers. The cry was heralded by the piccaninny light as it touched the scorched earth.

Women roused from sleep responded quickly and hurried to position themselves with their dogs in small groups behind the keening mourners.

Alarmed and with a thumping heart, I stepped out into the morning light and headed towards the wailing sorry group. As I neared the camp *Who, what, when?* raced through my mind; I captured a vision of Napanangka sitting in the red sand, tearing at her curly hair and striking her head. The smoke from her camp fire wafted around her head, creating a surreal halo.

I dropped to the ground beside her, taking her hand in mine.

'Who?' I asked.

She whispered, 'My sister, my sister.'

Suddenly I was swamped by a feeling of nauseating, gut-churning guilt. I recalled two weeks earlier that I had met Kumanjay in town. She was not her usual quiet self. She was drunk, sleeping rough, dirty and out of control. She wanted me to bring her home to the community. I wouldn't do it as she was drunk and disorderly.

The story unfolded that Kumanjay was found unconscious in the street. After a week in hospital she was ready for discharge on the day she died. The hospital doctor explained the cause of death to family members. They did not believe his white fella medical explanations.

Another patient saw a tall man at the end of Kumanjay's bed the night before she died. The tall man is a harbinger of death. The community knew that Kumanjay had been sung.

Later that day, Napanangka joined me in the clinic. She quickly depleted my supply of sterile scissors as she hacked at her hair until she resembled a porcupine. I followed behind her sweeping up her black locks. She asked me to burn them with the clinic rubbish to prevent any sorcerer finding the hair.

Following this ritual Napanangka said it was time to visit

Kumanjay's partner of twelve years, Boris, and tell him of her death. She asked me to drive her out to his camp as her sister was a poison relative to her husband, and even in death he could not be involved in any way. Not even to attend the funeral. I reluctantly agreed to her request, closed the clinic and we left.

Boris was a Vietnam vet who was rumoured to have post-traumatic stress. He camped on a remote desert gold lease which was protected by a legendary pack of savage dogs. On arrival at the lease, we were greeted by the baying pack.

Napanangka now told me that I had to tell Boris the news because it would not be proper for her culturally.

'What, Napanangka, that's a cop-out!' I said. 'You always drop the hard stuff on me claiming cultural immunity!'

Five ugly dogs snapped at the troopy wheels as we alighted. Napanangka headed off to the hut, leaving me standing alone sweating and tasting my terror. She looked over her shoulder and called me to come and ignore the dogs. I followed meekly. When we entered the hut, Napanangka stood in contemplation and then suddenly commenced spinning in circles, a black dervish, shouting loudly 'She's here. I feel her spirit,' while she raked at her scalp and tore at her hastily shorn hair.

I couldn't take my eyes off the guns stacked in the corner! A mental montage flashed through my mind. Take one Vietnam vet, add post-traumatic stress, rum, grief, anger, mix with my fear and stir with a gun!

Napanangka's voice cut through my thoughts and awakened Boris from his rum haze. His dogs barked and excitedly danced around Napanangka's spinning feet. After thirty years' abstinence I craved a cigarette, wished I could phone a friend!

Boris, a sad, toothless, lost soul of a man, stirred in his chair and looked up. He squinted, stared at me and coughed. After what seemed like an eternity he recognised me. He stood and clutched the table demanding to know, 'What's wrong?!' Thoughts tumbled through my mind as I tried to speak.

What's wrong, I thought, *Jesus, Mary and Joseph, could we could just start with the guns*!

Napanangka continued to spin out of control, crying out in language. She was haunted by her sister's spirit and its whispers. My hair stood on end as she hit a bed and finally collapsed on the floor keening and mumbling to herself. Between tears and wails she apportioned blame; identified guilty parties who would receive payback.

The words dead, passed away, last night, so sorry echoed around the hut. Was that really my voice I was hearing?

The words enveloped me as Boris roared. He swayed as he stood up and hurled his pannikin, striking the wall. He railed and screamed blame at me, family, Napanangka and others for his loss. When he was spent, he sat down and commenced sobbing loudly. My eyes never moved from the malevolent black gun barrels.

Finally fear and exhaustion overwhelmed me. I felt numb and became deaf to grief and keening. Taking deep breaths, I stumbled outside. Slowly I dug my fingers into the hot, red sand as crows arked noisily overhead in a bolt blue sky. The dogs joined me and sniffed as we eyeballed each other suspiciously.

Feeling that I had finally run out of psychic puff and had nothing left to give, I asked myself, was this a beginning or an end?

Napanangka woke me at 0600 by banging loudly on my door. She was unkempt and still wearing her two-week-old sorry camp clothes. She asked quietly for money to buy new black and white funeral clothes. I refused and she left, leaving me feeling guilty once more.

Arriving at the Australian Inland Mission chapel, I found it locked. The hearse was parked outside but no-one could locate the chapel key. Napanangka arrived resplendent in black and white with her blouse tag fluttering in the hot wind. She asked me to sit with her in the family pew between her and Boris.

Mourners stood under the solitary tree and shuffled patiently in the dusty heat. Heads had melted off the plastic flowers that adorned the coffin. Finally the key was found and we followed the coffin into the stifling chapel.

The service was well underway when an uninvited drunken, wailing woman staggered through the chapel side door and headed for the coffin. She launched herself towards the coffin and threw herself onto it and commenced rubbing her pendulous breasts up and down the length of the coffin lid.

To my astonishment neither mourners nor the pastor in the chapel stirred in protest. Instead I heard a collective sucking in of breath as the coffin and stand rocked and swayed perilously under her drunken weight. The only audible response was a deep growl from my dog, Wungadear, lying under the pew.

Her impromptu performance continued until she was joined by her drunken companion, who called to her in language, as he staggered through the side door. Suddenly she halted her wailing and breast rubbing, looked at the mourners with a bewildered expression and then unsteadily joined her companion. It was a wordless leaving, without their flies, which remained in the chapel, joining the larger mob buzzing round mourners' heads. The silence in the chapel was broken as the organist struck up a fractured version of 'Rock of Ages' followed by a swell of voices.

The colourful cortége of resilient desert Falcons and government four-wheel drives proceeded uneventfully to the nearby cemetery. Standing at the graveside, tears started to build up in my eyes. The emotional culmination of the past two weeks hit home. My sadness was abruptly broken by a strong elbow pushing me towards the grave edge; I was alarmed at first, until family members signed they wanted me to cast the first handful of red earth into the grave.

It landed with a dull thud and was rapidly followed by black hands in unison. The male cousin brothers shared their shovels and quickly filled the grave. No-one seemed to mind when Wungadear sprayed on the red mound adorned with artificial flowers.

Then, as if by silent command, the family, cousin brothers and mourners stopped keening, turned as a winged flock and faded as one. Napanangka and I stood quietly for a while then followed in their tracks.

There was no wake to follow with cucumber sangas and tea, or a piss-up at the local pub. I reflected how different black fella/white fella funerals were. No red-faced white fellas, sweating in tight suits, feigning care and directing mourners to sign a memorial book. Why would they need a book with a living memory that goes back 60 000 years?

Later that afternoon Napanangka and I travelled back in silence along the rough track to the community, each of us lost in our own wordless thoughts. Contemplating the number of clapped-out cars sitting majestically beside the road, display-ing their endurance and wounds, impervious to desert and time, I wondered if they were symbolic of remote area nurses!

Napanangka and Wungadear slept soundly while I opened and closed numerous gates. As the sun dropped behind red dunes, we arrived in the cool of the evening to a quiet, deserted community.

Marcel Corinne Campbell, registered nurse (remote)

chapter nine

FUTURE
PATHWAYS

---

*Forging their way forward, women and men, both older
and younger, are creating pathways to ensure both their
professional development and ongoing nursing services in
the changing landscape of rural and remote Australia.*

Cultivating
Community Health
REMOTE AUSTRALIA

I have been intrigued with cross-cultural issues since my early student nursing days, studying Medical Anthropology in Canada, way back in the late '70s. This cultural intrigue, particularly relating to maternal and child health, took me to the UK to complete a Diploma in Midwifery and eventually, to the far reaches of the Arctic (the North West Territories of Canada) in 1988 and the Australian outback (Northern Territory, East Arnhem Land) in the early 1990s.

I feel that community health is where health begins for any cultural group. Consequently, I have 'armed' myself with some of the necessary bits and pieces to do what I feel is my job as a remote area nurse (RAN) and midwife, but an RAN's learning doesn't stop. I have a list a mile long of the courses that I would like to take, including the CRANA*plus* Remote Emergency Care course, because immediate emergency care knowledge and confidence can make or break a good RAN and I do like sleeping peacefully at night when on call.

As my daughter grew up, I spent time working as an agency hospital and community-based midwife and nurse in various capacities: community liaison, hospital and community midwifery; sexual and reproductive health; educator; community nurse and; of course, as an RAN.

As you can imagine, each cultural group that I had the joy and honour of working with was so very different in so many ways: caring for the needs of Indigenous street kids in downtown Brisbane is very different from the work in Fort McPherson in Canada, Milingimbi in the Northern Territory, Oak Valley in South Australia or Cherbourg in Queensland.

All have their differences and individual challenges. Despite some obvious similarities, picking wild berries in northern Canada with the women and children while the men stood guard with an eye open for hungry bears is very different from hunting for mangrove worms and crabs in East Arnhem Land while keeping an eye out for hungry crocodiles. However, on reflection, I have realised that the basic needs of all communities are the same: we all share the need to eat good food to keep us strong and the need to remain safe in our environment.

So what role does a remote area nurse play in facilitating this? Especially in communities that are struggling with cultural change? I have asked myself that question a million times and the answer I sought wasn't in the books I read or the teachers and 'wise ones' that I studied under. It isn't so much about giving out medicine or doing health checks. It also isn't about doing 'on call' or handing out pamphlets that talk about well women screening. And it isn't about telling a community how they should 'do it'.

It's in the sharing and caring; the day-to-day 'stuff'. It's caring about a mother who is struggling to feed her babies good tucker or who lives in isolation from her family when her husband abandons her. It's caring about a young man who knows he'll probably never be a rock star or make enough money to buy that fancy car he sees driving through the city streets on

TV. It's about caring for that young sick child who is so afraid when she sees you holding that needle with penicillin in it.

It's in the compassion, the comradeship, the feeling of being part of a bigger whole; sharing an orange with the little kid with big eyes when you're on your lunch break. It's in stopping long enough in your busy day to share a laugh with the women who are clustered around the health clinic waiting to see the doctor or child health nurse. It's in the tears that are shed when a family is in sorry business for a grandmother who passes away far from her home and people who love her.

It's about 'both way' learning; about watching and being with people in their environment and learning about how they 'do it'. It's about attending ceremonies if appropriate and going hunting for bush foods. It's about learning about bush medicine (and using it). It's about listening to language and trying out a few words, then using those words and adding to them when you care for the people.

Life as an RAN is full; rarely is there a dull moment and you can get really tired and downhearted. I like to take a break every once in a while just to get a feeling of self; to hang out with my family and maybe have a soy latte at my favourite café. Sometimes I go on a retreat to re-establish who I am and what I want from life.

As an RAN, I also feel very strongly that it is important not to take myself too seriously. All I can do is my best at any given moment; I need to know my boundaries and on occasion, I need to laugh at my shortcomings. After all, laughter *is* the best medicine for any community in any culture.

Tere Garnons-Williams, remote area nurse and midwife

Finding My Place

CENTRAL AUSTRALIA

I was working in Adelaide in the emergency department of a tertiary referral hospital. I was there for nearly seven years and I got burnt out. I didn't recognise it as I loved my job and thought everything was fine but my wife, Anita, saw the signs and wasn't going to put up with it. She said either I quit or she was leaving. Next day I signed up with an agency. I gradually worked further and further out of the metropolitan area and one day I was driving home listening to music and there was a song that came on about a bushman not being able to survive in the city, and I just burst into tears and realised I couldn't do this any more. I realised I had to get out of the city and back to the bush.

I grew up on the Eyre Peninsula and my intention was always to go to Adelaide, get an education and then go back to the country because so many people didn't go back but I always wanted to. That day in the traffic was my watershed moment so I started looking for jobs in the country. A position at Oodnadatta in the north of South Australia came up and so I uprooted my city-born wife and small daughters and moved them 1100 kilometres north into the desert. That was our first real taste of outback life. It was an amazing experience.

Making the transition was a bit challenging for Anita as she had had her own career path in Adelaide, but she did a nursing refresher course and then was able to get a job at the Coober Pedy Hospital 200 kilometres away. She went over there for two shifts a week, staying the night in between.

The most significant impact for me arriving in Oodnadatta was the realisation that I was completely unprepared for the work. I had thought because I worked in emergency I'd be able to handle anything but, in fact, emergency was only about five per cent of the work. The rest was primary health care and health promotion and I had no experience in either. I didn't know where to start so that's when I started my professional development. I went on to get a Master of Remote Health Practice and converted it into a Nurse Practitioner Masters and a Master of Remote Health Management. I really wanted to know how to do this job the best way that I could.

I started that study while I was at Oodnadatta, but then we got pregnant with our third child and Anita was diagnosed with multiple sclerosis (MS). We'd been advised not to give birth out in the bush so we moved in to Alice Springs for twelve months and then to Hermannsburg community, about an hour out of Alice. I started out there as one of the remote area nurses in the clinic and then within six months I was promoted to manager, a job I held for the next four years.

We'd always known we'd have to move into a bigger community as Anita's MS progressed, so we moved to Tennant Creek and I work as one of the team in the emergency department at the hospital. Anita is in a wheelchair now and so working in a team situation gives me the opportunity to keep working as well as provide Anita with the assistance she needs.

Ultimately, I would like to go back to remote area nursing. My dream job would be working as a nurse practitioner in a remote Aboriginal community. I like the sense of independence and autonomy that goes with that role and the opportunity not to be constrained by frustrating rules. You have broad guidelines to work in but within those broad guidelines there's a lot of area for exercising clinical judgement and that's very satisfying.

It's also the most money you can earn as a registered nurse in Australia; sometimes that's built on exorbitant amounts of overtime and that can be very wearing, but the money is a big drawcard and we can't pretend that it's not a factor. It is a part of the attraction.

Then there's the fact that it is community work and you'd probably find that people who work in community settings have higher levels of satisfaction with their work compared to people who work in hospital wards. I know that's certainly the case for me.

The thing is, when I started out as a nurse, I saw it as a step towards eventually doing medicine, but I made the choice to get married and have a family instead. Working as a nurse practitioner is a great compromise.

John Wright, registered nurse (remote)

Training Up

ALICE SPRINGS, NORTHERN TERRITORY

As the Aboriginal support coordinator for CRANA*plus*, I go to the communities and talk to the elders about new nurses getting deployed there. I introduce the nurse to the elders and they'll give him/her the cultural awareness of the community they're in. I liaise between the workers and the elders. A lot of them are just there for a week or two from one of the agencies and then they go somewhere else. At the moment I work with nine communities in the Central Desert area of the Northern Territory.

I am also training as an Aboriginal health practitioner. I've been pushed by others to do my Cert IV so that I can facilitate some of the training programs like Remote Emergency Care and First Line Emergency Care, which incorporates Maternity Emergency Care and Advanced Emergency Support.

I live in Alice Springs but I was born in Victoria, at Echuca, and I'm a Yorta Yorta man. I've worked in the Central Desert area for a long time and get along well with everyone around there. There are not many male health workers out there and there is a big need so I'll work two or three days in the communities and facilitate the courses in between. I'll go where I'm needed.

The biggest challenges for men are diabetes and renal, same as the women. I've seen blokes lose limbs because they haven't had help with their medication and stuff. It's just a matter of talking to them and telling them this will help you get better and then make sure they take it.

One of the things I'll do is push young people to do the Batchelor (Batchelor Institute of Indigenous Tertiary Education, about an hour south of Darwin) courses like I'm doing and become Aboriginal health practitioners. Especially the young males, who are running around with nothing to do. With national registration, that bit of paper will give them a chance at a job wherever they are. Most of the young people have only done primary school education; they don't get to high school because most of the communities don't have high school, so they can't get into other training. Health is one of the things they can get into and doing Cert IV gives them a chance to go up the ladder. In the course I'm in now, there are three men and one of them is going to go on and train in nursing. There are ten women in the course as well.

I'm really enjoying my job and the training. I did some clinical practice with Jo Appo (a well-experienced Aboriginal clinical health practitioner) recently. A young fellow came in with scabies and she said, 'Well, go on, you deal with it,' and so I told him what I was going to do and did it. It was great. Being a health worker is something you can do for as long as you like so it's a good thing to be doing.

Lenny Cooper, Aboriginal health practitioner and Aboriginal Support Coordinator for CRANAplus

Now They See

TENNANT CREEK, NORTHERN TERRITORY

When I started working as the Barkly Regional Eye Health Coordinator for Anyinginyi Health Aboriginal Corporation in 2006, many Aboriginal people in Tennant Creek did not expect to be able to see well as they aged. In some cases, they expected to lose their eyesight completely.

There had not been an Eye Coordinator for a year, visits

from optometrists were not frequent and many people just couldn't afford to buy glasses. Now we have a one-stop shop for eye care thanks to a partnership with an eye specialist, Dr Henderson, who has been coming to Tennant Creek for the last twelve years, the Brien Holden Vision Institute (BHVI), OPSM, Tennant Creek Hospital, the Royal Flying Doctor Service, Fred Hollows Foundation and Alice Springs Hospital.

Back in 2006, I had no car, no permanent clinic and no help. Now I have a car, a permanent clinic and an assistant. Dr Henderson comes here from Alice Springs every two months for four days. On one of those days he operates on all sorts of eye conditions, including cataracts, entropions (the eyelid folds inward causing the lashes to rub against the cornea) and pterygia (a membrane that invades the cornea). He is known for not only his medical and surgical skills but also his compassion and empathy with all patients.

We have had so many successes as a result of this collaborative initiative. For instance, one of our senior Aboriginal ladies had been a very good hunter in her younger days but due to cataracts, she suffered loss of vision in her one good eye and had to be cared for by her family. With a lot of talking and the help of others, an appointment was made and she was quickly referred to Dr Henderson. He operated on her on a Tuesday, the pad came off the eye on the Wednesday and she went hunting and caught four goannas on a Saturday. The next week she caught four echidnas.

Many Aboriginal people here continue to maintain many traditional ways, including hunting and using bush medicines. These aspects of their lives are only improved with better sight.

I was fortunate, after I took on the role, to hear about

BHVI, which provides easily accessible optometrists. The institute's involvement in Tennant Creek has increased visits from optometrists fourteen-fold. They also provided subsidised glasses, a service now taken over by the Fred Hollows Foundation. This system has allowed people to pay for glasses out of Centrelink payments or wages, meaning affordable glasses for all.

It has been wonderful to be involved in helping to create this one-stop shop which provides a cohesive, safe delivery of eye care. We see babies, children, teenagers, young adults and those of more senior years. We are very happy that we have been part of helping Aboriginal artists to keep doing their outstanding work. People not only come to us for help, but they are also referred to us by doctors, nurses, AHWs, other Aboriginal people and family members.

One gentleman who had cataracts in both eyes needed to be cared for by two people. Four months after he had his operation, I could not find him for his next check. I was delighted to find that he was no longer housebound and was travelling the country seeing family and doing what he wanted.

The changes in some people's lives have been huge.

Maree O'Hara, registered nurse and coordinator, Barkly Regional Eye Health

Learning the Ropes

UTOPIA, NORTHERN TERRITORY

For a second-year student nurse I don't think you can get a more culturally invigorating clinical placement than going out on a remote prac. Every sense is awakened and your clinical skills are pushed to new limits. Up until now my clinical nursing experience was bound to large metropolitan hospitals. Going to the Urapuntja Health Service (UHS) in Utopia, about 280 kilometres north-east of Alice Springs, was both eye-opening and refreshing.

Set up in the 1970s on the decentralised community model, UHS is a community-controlled Aboriginal medical service. Monday to Thursday we would go with the nurses and sometimes a doctor or an Aboriginal health worker, out over the dirt roads to the different communities in the area.

It was such beautiful country with wild flowers and desert shrubs contrasting brilliantly with the bright-red soil. They had a lot of rain last season so the desert was blooming and was full of life.

When we arrived at an outstation we would set up a little clinic out the back of the four-wheeled drive. It was quite well equipped with medication boxes, tables, chairs, computers and supplies. People would come to get a health check, their medications or anything else they needed. I was totally blown away by this different take on health care. It was community and patient centred, and the nurses all had their own ways of connecting with their clients. It was great to see the mix of skills and life experience that brings people to this kind of nursing.

Being out in the desert really emphasised what a diverse and rewarding profession nursing is. We were able to see how another culture lived; their way of life and how health and illness impacted on the community. It was a real privilege to see and be included. All the staff at Urapuntja promoted a holistic approach to health care, which encouraged local healing remedies such as bush medicine coupled with the western biomedical approach.

The biggest challenge that I found was the language barrier; I wasn't expecting it to be so vast. I was impressed and inspired by how the health professionals were able to give comprehensive and quality care despite the language difficulties. They used basic words and gestures to explain what was happening to their bodies and to communicate what medical intervention needed to happen.

This experience has changed my view on health care delivery in Australia. It has reinforced how vital holistic care is and how nurses can influence the lives of so many people across the country. I was very lucky to have a sneak peek at what it is like to be a remote area nurse and it has definitely inspired me to pursue future education pathways that will allow me to explore this great, wide country using my nursing skills.

Ely Taylor, student nurse, Emerging Nurse Leader Program

Stock Camp Nurse

NORTH-WEST QUEENSLAND

My love for north-west Queensland began when I worked in the stock camp of Miranda Downs, a cattle station near Normanton. I've heard people slander romantic stories of the outback; however, nothing could be further from the truth in my experience.

Each morning as we headed out in the horse truck, I recall staring out the window, dreamily contemplating the day ahead and about working shoulder to shoulder with the rest of the crew. The days were full of banter, bulls and bullshit and I was surrounded by a team that worked like a well-oiled machine. Whether it all went right or all went wrong, or somewhere in between, we'd climb back into the truck at the end of the day sitting shoulder to shoulder again as the sun dropped down. Does it get more romantic than that?

Apparently it does. I met my fiancé Quinton Jurd that year at Miranda Downs. He currently runs the stock camp on another cattle station three hours north of Mount Isa. The crew in the stock camp undertake all the cattle mustering for the station throughout the dry months of the year. I try to visit as often as possible.

For the last three years, I have been studying in Melbourne to complete my Bachelor of Nursing at Australian Catholic Uni. Each time I journey to north-west Queensland, I feel as though I am returning home. As such, I organised to complete my final nursing placement in Mount Isa.

The Mount Isa hospital draws patients from a radius of 300 000 square kilometres. Last year, I was fortunate to be placed on the surgical ward of the hospital for a five-week prac for my final year of nursing. The Mount Isa Centre for Rural and Remote Health provided orientation and cultural awareness training before I began placement on the surgical ward.

The fly-in-fly-out mining workforce, backpackers and grey nomads make the provision of health care increasingly complex as many travel into the region from interstate, and therefore, request interstate transfers.

I was shocked at how often people required transfers to Townsville or to return to their home town. Another challenge involved people getting transfers in from an outlying community then not presenting to the hospital for their admission or their appointment.

I had an incredibly positive experience and was able to achieve all of my placement goals. Overall, it was the staff on the ward that ensured I looked forward to placement every day. I was fortunate to have been accepted into the 2013 North West Health Service graduate nurse program and I am loving both my job and being back in the area full-time.

Balancing my life as a nurse with my other life out in the stock camp with Quinton provides me with the best possible lifestyle. We are both passionate about our careers and envisage living and working in remote Australia for the foreseeable future. We have dreams of travelling across the country, the ringer and the nurse!

Catherine Ryan, registered nurse (a member of the Emerging Nurse Leader Program)

Acknowledgements

The plan for this book was to publish a collection of stories either from or about rural and remote nurses and to raise some money for a worthy cause. Frontier Services was chosen as the worthy recipient in acknowledgement of their 100 years of service to inland Australia.

It was publisher Andrea McNamara who got the ball rolling for this project. Thank you for asking me to edit this book, Andrea – it's an opportunity for which I will be forever grateful. One of the first conversations I had with her was about my concern that nurses would be reluctant and/or too busy to write their stories, assuming I could track down enough of them in the first place. My networks around the outback are pretty good but I'd never have managed this without Anne-Marie Bourchers and Geri Malone from CRANA*plus*. Anne-Marie, in particular, promoted the call for stories through their magazine, encouraged everyone she knew to participate and made it possible for me to attend the 2012 CRANA*plus* conference in Cairns, a captive audience of rural and remote nurses from all around Australia. Her grace in the face of my endless requests for contact details was remarkable.

I would also like to thank editor Adrian Potts – he has been a dream to work with and I hope we work together for long enough to become great friends! I must also extend my gratitude to editor Brooke Clark, and to editor Bridget Maidment, who first made contact with me about this project.

Finally, my heartfelt thanks go to the nurses who contributed their stories to this collection and to the people who wrote about the special nurses in their lives.

Thank you for sharing your stories.

Frontier Services

The Australian Inland Mission (AIM) was established in 1912 by Rev. John Flynn. Having researched the needs of both Aboriginal and European inhabitants of the inland of Australia, on behalf of the Presbyterian Church of Australia, he was appointed Superintendent of the AIM and tasked with bringing appropriate medical and spiritual services to the outback.

In 1977 the AIM became known as Frontier Services. Between them, the first nursing sisters and patrol padres picked up the creation threads of Flynn's 'mantle of safety'. A complex invisible fabric of medical, spiritual, social, cultural and economic service provision, the 'mantle' has been stitched together with compassion, empathy, determination, dedication, guts and the sheer goodwill of all the people who have ever worked for or supported the work of the Australian Inland Mission/Frontier Services.

In recognition of their centenary in 2012, Penguin is delighted to contribute the royalties from *Bush Nurses* to Frontier Services.

CRANA*plus*

The Council of Remote Area Nurses of Australia (CRANA) was formed in 1983 when 130 remote area nurses from across Australia came together in Alice Springs to put remote health issues on the national agenda. General concern about the poor health status of people who live in remote areas and the inequities, quality and accessibility in services available to these Australians was and remains the catalyst for action.

In 2008, members voted to extend membership to all remote health professionals and their supporters, reflecting the collaborative nature of remote area nursing, which works closely with other professions to meet the challenges of remote health. The name was then changed to CRANA*plus* to reflect the new broadened scope of the organisation.

The core business and sole focus of CRANA*plus* is to educate, support and advocate for all health professionals working in the remote sector of Australia.

crana.org.au

Bush Support Services

Due to their isolation, be it geographic, social and/or environmental, remote area health workers face chronically high levels of occupational stress. These same workers also face increased chances of experiencing discrete traumatic events. The Bush Support Services (BSS) was established in 1997 and is currently funded by the Commonwealth Department of Health and Ageing and auspiced by CRANA*plus*. The BSS is staffed by eight highly trained and experienced psychologists, supported by two administrative staff.

Understanding that both Indigenous and non-Indigenous remote health workers have particular mental health needs, the BSS provides a free and confidential telephone counselling, debriefing and support service. In addition, BSS provides educational packages and outreaches to remote area workers by running fun activities such as a stress-buster competition and a knitting project.

Sometimes, it's just about having someone safe to off-load to, so if you're a remote health worker or the family of one and you feel like a chat, call Bush Support Services.

bss.crana.org.au
Phone counselling 1800 805391
Email counselling: scp@crana.org.au